Peterson
First Guide

to

WILDFLOWERS
of Northeastern and North-central

North America

Roger Tory Peterson

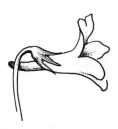

HOUGHTON
MIFFLIN
COMPANY

·

BOSTON
1986

Selected illustrations reproduced from *A Field Guide to
Wildflowers of Northeastern and North-central North
America*, copyright © 1968 by Roger Tory Peterson and
Margaret McKenny.

Illustrations that appeared in black and white in *A Field
Guide to Wildflowers* were colored for the *First Guide*
by Gordon Morrison.

Library of Congress Cataloging-in-Publication Data

Peterson, Roger Tory, date
Peterson First guide to wildflowers of northeastern
and north-central North America.

Includes index.
1. Wild flowers—Northeastern States—Identification.
2. Wild flowers—Middle West—Identification.   I. Title.
II. Title: First guide to wildflowers of northeastern
and north-central North America.
QK118.P526   1986   582.13′0974   85-27224
ISBN 0-395-40777-X

Printed in Italy

NI 10 9 8 7 6 5 4 3 2 1

INTRODUCING THE WILDFLOWERS

One of my bird-watching friends once sent me a little book, *How to Tell the Birds From the Flowers.* I don't recall it clearly, but it was illustrated with Edward Lear-like line drawings showing how to tell a crow from a crocus, a plover from a clover, a catbird from catnip, a cowbird from a cowslip, a sparrow from asparagus, and a hawk from a hollyhock.

Indeed, this amusing spoof seemed to reflect the couldn't-care-less attitude of my friend about flowers. This attitude is not shared by most nature-oriented people, but they often complain, "There are just too many kinds. Where do we start?" True, there are many more kinds of flowers to deal with than there are birds. This soon becomes apparent when you open the pages of the standard technical botanies such as *The New Britain and Brown Illustrated Flora*, updated by Dr. Henry A. Gleason, who describes 4,460 flowering plants and ferns in the northeastern and north-central quarter of North America. Gray's *Manual of Botany*, updated by Professor M.L. Fernald, puts the figure even higher, at 5,520. This is because these two authorities differ about some of the fine points of taxonomy—whether a flower deserves recognition as a valid species, or not.

As a young person interested in birds, but wishing to extend my natural history horizons, I waded through the formal keys in the various botanies, and as often as not I was bewildered. Being a visual person, trained as an artist, I preferred the picture-matching approach.

It was the visual point of view that inspired my *Field Guide to the Birds*, wherein live birds are described by their patterns, shapes, and the special "field marks" that can be seen at a distance, rather than the technical points specialists use to name species in the hand or in the specimen tray.

In fact, in those earlier days when we were just emerging from the shotgun era of ornithology, some museum curators were badly outclassed by amateur birdwatchers who used only their binoculars. I soon found that some professional botanists (not all) also moved about in a rarified atmosphere and could tell a flower with more certainty after it was pressed and mounted on an herbarium sheet than they could when the plant was alive and growing. The vasculum (collecting case) and hand lens were their tools.

Many years ago, my friend, the late Margaret McKenny, then Secretary to the City Garden Club of New York, and I discussed this dilemma. Thus we conceived our *Field Guide to Wildflowers of Northeastern and North-central North America*, a visual approach to identification based on color, form, and detail, using the little arrows that had become the trademark of the "Peterson System."

We reasoned that it would be impossible to describe and illustrate all of the several thousand species in a single volume smaller than a good-sized telephone directory. Even if this could be done, the average layman would be reluctant to face such a formidable galaxy, so we decided on a selective approach. But even so, what a staggering commitment! Eventually, over a period of nearly 20 years, I made well over 1,500 drawings of flowers— 1,344 of which appeared in the *Field Guide.* I covered thousands of miles by car in the eastern and midland states, trying to catch the brief periods of bloom of various species.

My battered vasculum was crammed with my finds; eventually I switched to plastic bags that served to trap moisture more effectively than the enameled tin box. In the case of orchids and other endangered flowers, I did not pick them; I drew them while lying on the ground, or else I took photographs from which I could draw later. But most of the flowers, still quite fresh, were drawn in the evening in tourist cabins and motels.

Before she returned to her home in the West, Margaret McKenny wrote the first draft of what was to have been the running text. This covered about 650 species. My own part, aside from the drawings, was to prepare the abbreviated text opposite the illustrations. After her initial text was written we realized that the number of species covered was not sufficient. I eventually drew 1,300 species, which created another problem. Space would not permit the full cross-referenced treatment between the running text and the legend pages. The solution was to prepare a more telegraphic text, self-contained, opposite the illustrations. This rewrite and the preparation of the additional 650 entries became my responsibility. When the book finally saw the light of day it became an immediate success and has remained so.

Even though the book is intended for the novice, there are still many beginners, who can name few flowers other than a dandelion, a buttercup, and a daisy, who would like something even simpler to start with—a smaller guide that would give them confidence. Because of this need, the publisher of the *Field Guides*, Houghton Mifflin, urged me to prepare this *First Guide to Wildflowers*. As in the *First Guide to Birds*, I have selected about 200 species and prepared a new text. My illustrations have been borrowed from the *Field Guide*; those which were in black and white are now in color.

Area Covered: This little book is only an introduction, primarily useful in the eastern and midwestern states and adjacent Canada. The main thrust is toward those flowers that are most likely to attract the attention of the beginner, especially the flowers of the spring woodlands and the flowers of the roadsides and suburban edges.

As for the spring flowers, they are a celebration of vibrant life when they carpet the floor of the woodlands before the trees leaf out. They are native species. On the other hand, most of the flowers of the roadside are alien plants, brought over from Europe. A roadside is a roadside the world over, so those flowers that have been able to survive in the disturbed soils of the Old World also do very well here. They offer us much beauty in the guise of daisies, Chicory, Bouncing Bet, Day-lilies, Queen Anne's Lace, Yarrow, the clovers, and a host of others. Indeed, what would our roadsides and waste places be without them? They should not be despised as "weeds."

How to Start

When you find a new plant, note the type of flower. How many petals does it have? Are the flowers single, in pairs, loose groups, or in tight clusters? Are the leaves toothed or not; are they opposite each other on the stem, or alternate? Is the plant smooth or hairy? Familiarize yourself with the shapes of flowers and leaves as shown on the following pages. Memorize the terms.

This *"First"* guide is only a sampling to get you started. You will soon be ready for the full treatment, with one of the *Field Guides* listed below:

A Field Guide to Wildflowers of Northeastern and North-central North America by Roger Tory Peterson and Margaret McKenny

A Field Guide to Rocky Mountain Wildflowers by John J. Craighead, Frank C. Craighead, Jr., and Ray J. Davis

A Field Guide to Pacific States Wildflowers by Theodore F. Niehaus and Charles L. Ripper

A Field Guide to Southwestern and Texas Wildflowers by Theodore F. Niehaus, Charles L. Ripper, and Virginia Savage

A Field Guide to Wildflowers Coloring Book by Roger Tory Peterson and Frances Tenenbaum is also available.

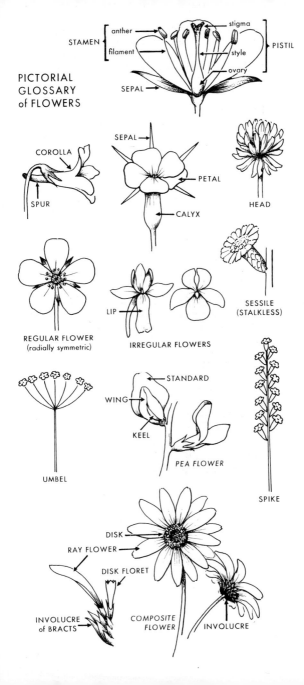

PICTORIAL GLOSSARY of FLOWERS

STAMEN — anther, filament
PISTIL — stigma, style, ovary
SEPAL

COROLLA
SPUR

SEPAL
PETAL
CALYX

HEAD

REGULAR FLOWER
(radially symmetric)

LIP

IRREGULAR FLOWERS

SESSILE
(STALKLESS)

UMBEL

STANDARD
WING
KEEL
PEA FLOWER

SPIKE

DISK
RAY FLOWER
DISK FLORET
INVOLUCRE
of BRACTS
COMPOSITE
FLOWER
INVOLUCRE

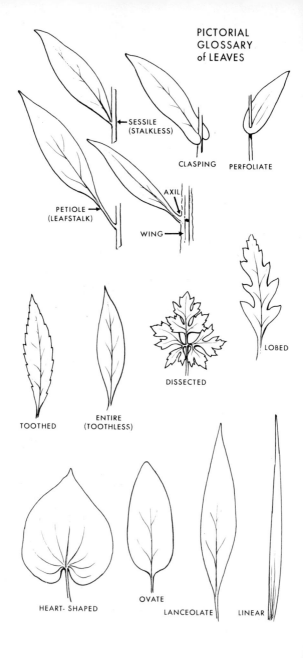

PICTORIAL GLOSSARY of LEAVES

SESSILE (STALKLESS)

CLASPING

PERFOLIATE

PETIOLE (LEAFSTALK)

AXIL

WING

TOOTHED

ENTIRE (TOOTHLESS)

DISSECTED

LOBED

HEART-SHAPED

OVATE

LANCEOLATE

LINEAR

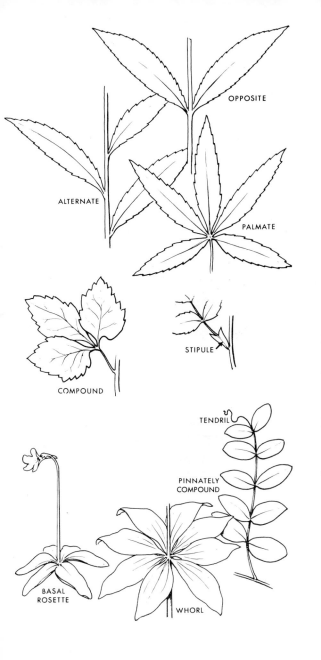

OPPOSITE

ALTERNATE

PALMATE

COMPOUND

STIPULE

TENDRIL

PINNATELY
COMPOUND

BASAL
ROSETTE

WHORL

MAY-APPLE, MANDRAKE
Barberry Family
May-apples have large, glossy leaves that
often form carpetlike colonies in woodland
openings. The 2 *deeply divided, umbrella-
like* leaves all but conceal the nodding,
waxy white flower that *hugs the stem*. The
flower (April to May) is followed by a
large, lemonlike berry. The leaves, roots,
and seeds are poisonous, but the fruit
is edible and can be made into jelly.

BLOODROOT
Poppy Family
Blooming at about the same time
(March–May) as the Hepatica (p. 86), the
Bloodroot opens its single cuplike white
flower to greet the spring. A large, pale,
lobed leaf embraces the 6- to 10-inch
stalk. If the stem is broken an *orange juice*
oozes forth. Bloodroot is found in rich
woodlands.

BUNCHBERRY, DWARF CORNEL
Dogwood Family
Believe it or not, the Bunchberry, only 3 to
8 inches tall, belongs to the same genus
as the Flowering Dogwood, which may grow
to 30 or 40 feet. The *4 showy white
"petals"* are really *bracts;* the real flowers
are tiny, forming a greenish cluster at the
center of the bracts, which surmount the
whorl of 6 glossy leaves. The Bunchberry
presents its floral show in cool woods from
May to July. In autumn tight clusters of
scarlet berries appear.

LARGE-FLOWERED TRILLIUM
Lily Family
Few other spring flowers are as showy. As
in other trilliums, *all the parts*—leaves,
petals, and sepals—*are in 3's.* The white
flowers, 2 to 4 inches across, turn pinkish
with age. It prefers rich soil. Before the
trees leaf out, some woodlands are literally
carpeted with its white blossoms and green
leaves.

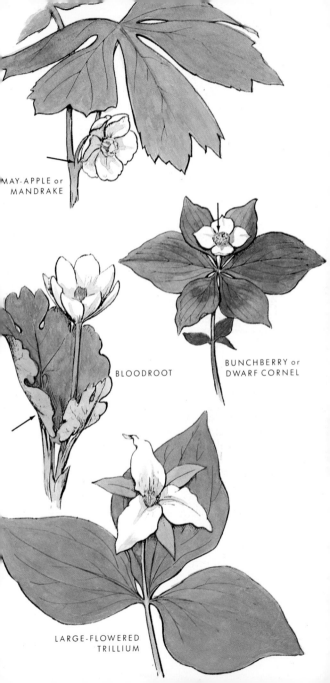

MAY-APPLE or
MANDRAKE

BLOODROOT

BUNCHBERRY or
DWARF CORNEL

LARGE-FLOWERED
TRILLIUM

FRAGRANT WATER-LILY
Water-lily Family

This immaculate beauty of the ponds and quiet waters floats among *large, platterlike leaves* that are anchored to the muddy bottom by long, immersed stems. If you lift these floating leaves with your canoe paddle, you will find that they are *purplish* beneath. The multi-petaled flowers, 3 to 5 inches across, have a *pungent fragrance*, attractive (no doubt) to pollinating insects. The Fragrant Water-lily blooms all summer long, from Manitoba and Newfoundland southward through the eastern and central states. A similar species, the **Tuberous Water-lily** (not shown), found west of the Appalachians, has more broadly rounded petals. The flowers are not fragrant and the leaves are usually green below, not purplish.

BROAD-LEAVED ARROWHEAD
Arrowhead Family

Three roundish petals and the arrangement of the flowers in whorls of 3 are typical of the arrowheads, as are the *arrow-shaped leaves;* some of the plants in this family have leaves that are lancelike or grasslike. There are 16 species in our area, 8 of which are covered in *A Field Guide to Wildflowers.* From July to October the Broad-leaved Arrowhead opens its triads of *white* flowers at the pond edge or above the shallow water of lakes and ponds throughout our area. Edges of ponds where water-lilies grow in profusion are often punctuated by the slim spikes of arrowheads. By contrast, Pickerelweed, which also has arrowhead-shaped leaves, sends up tight spikes of *blue* flowers (see p. 109).

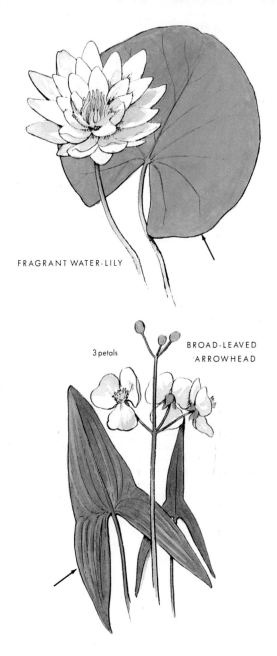

FRAGRANT WATER-LILY

3 petals

BROAD-LEAVED
ARROWHEAD

HEDGE BINDWEED
Morning-glory Family

Superficially, this attractive wild morning-glory looks like the next species, but note the *arrowhead-shaped* or *spade-shaped leaves*. The flowers, which may be white or pink, bloom from May to September in thickets and roadside tangles over much of our area. There are a number of other kinds of wild morning-glories. Especially noteworthy is the **Upright** or **Low Bindweed** (not shown), a short, erect plant with *oval leaves*. It is less than a foot tall and *does not trail* like a vine as do the others.

WILD POTATO-VINE
Morning-glory Family

In spite of its name, this is a true morning-glory. It can be separated from the similar Hedge Bindweed (above) by its *heart-shaped leaves*. The large, bell-like flowers, 2–3 inches across, are white with pink stripes radiating from the center. Like most other plants in its family, the Wild Potato-vine is a trailing vine that may climb over low shrubs and fenceposts. It blooms throughout the summer, in the dry soil of field edges and roadsides from Michigan, southern Ontario, New York, and Connecticut southward.

JAPANESE HONEYSUCKLE
Honeysuckle Family

This weedy vine, an alien, is difficult to get rid of once it takes hold in thickets and along roadsides, where it covers the ground and bushes with its winding stems and evergreen foliage. The flowers, with their *long projecting stamens*, may be white or buffy. These develop later into *black berries*. The Japanese Honeysuckle blossoms from April to July, from the southern Great Lakes states and Massachusetts southward.

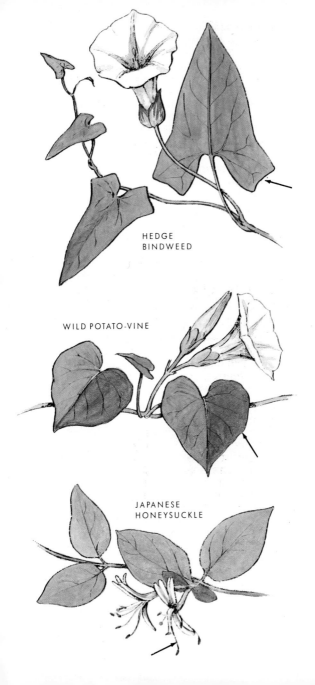

HEDGE
BINDWEED

WILD POTATO-VINE

JAPANESE
HONEYSUCKLE

WOOD ANEMONE
Buttercup Family

The Wood Anemone, with its 5 (or more) white, petal-like sepals, is only 4 to 5 inches high. Like the **Rue-anemone** (not shown), it might be overlooked among the galaxy of other spring flowers that carpet the open woodlands. It differs from the Rue-anemone in having a whorl of *deeply cut*, 3-parted (or sometimes 5-parted) leaves midway on the stem.

COMMON WOOD-SORREL
Wood-sorrel Family

Note the *inversely heart-shaped, cloverlike* leaflets—"shamrocks." The flowers, each on a separate 3- or 4-inch stalk, are 5-petaled, white or pink, *veined with deeper pink*. The Wood-sorrel blooms from May to early July in cool woods. A related species, the **Violet Wood-sorrel** (not shown), is a bit larger. Its 5 flaring petals are *purplish violet*. The leaflets are reddish or purplish underneath.

DUTCHMAN'S-BREECHES
Poppy Family   (Bleeding Heart Subfamily)

As one might suspect, this attractive springtime flower is related to the familiar Bleeding Heart of the garden. The several waxy, yellow-tipped flowers droop from an arched stem. Each flower has *a pair of hollow spurs* that suggest tiny pantaloons "ankles up." The leaves are much dissected, almost fernlike. This delicate plant blooms in April and May in rich woodlands.

STARFLOWER
Poppy Family

In the cool woods and mountain slopes in late spring the Starflower opens its *pairs of fragile white flowers*. The two 6- to 7-pointed stars are supported by *threadlike stalks* that surmount a whorl of 5 to 9 long, tapering leaves. This is a small plant, seldom more than 5 or 6 inches in height.

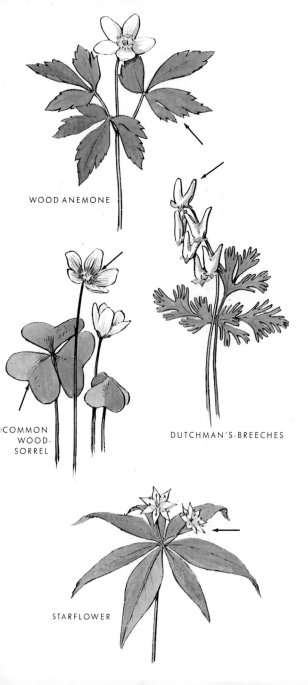

WOOD ANEMONE

COMMON
WOOD-
SORREL

DUTCHMAN'S-BREECHES

STARFLOWER

CANADA VIOLET
Violet Family

Of the many violets, a majority are blue, but many are yellow or white. The Canada Violet, the most handsome of the white ones, stands on 8- to 16-inch purplish stems. Tell it from other white violets by the *back* of the petals, which are *purplish.* It blooms from April to June in southern Canada, the northern edge of the U.S., and the higher Appalachians. Eight other white violets are shown in *A Field Guide to Wildflowers.*

SPRING-BEAUTY
Purslane Family

This aptly named flower of the moist woods is suggestive of the wood-sorrels and wood anemones, but can be recognized by the pair of smooth, *linear leaves* halfway up the stem. The 5-petaled flowers are white or pink (see p. 87), with darker pink veins. Spring-beauties are among the earliest flowers to bloom, from March to May.

CAROLINA SPRING-BEAUTY
Purslane Family

This little flower of the spring woodlands is similar to the other Spring-beauty except for its leaves, which are *paddle-shaped* with *slender petioles.* In spite of its restrictive name, this flower is found from the Appalachians north to southern Canada and westward. Look for it from March to May.

DEWDROP
Rose Family

Rising from trailing roots, the Dewdrop sends up its small, *solitary,* bushy-stamened flower on a 2- to 5-inch *reddish stalk.* The *round, finely scalloped leaves* are on separate stalks. This dainty woodland flower blooms from June to August in southern Canada, adjacent U.S., and southward in the Appalachian highlands.

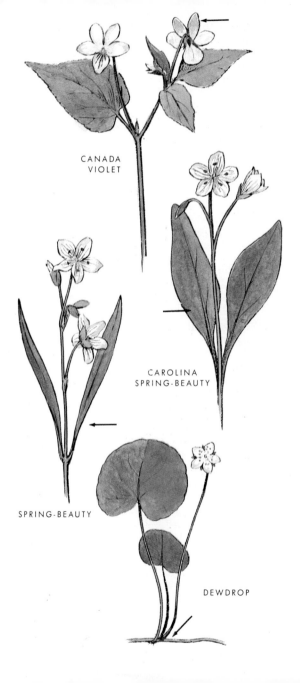

CANADA
VIOLET

CAROLINA
SPRING-BEAUTY

SPRING-BEAUTY

DEWDROP

BRAMBLES (BLACKBERRIES)
Rose Family

Most plants of the genus *Rubus*, to which blackberries and raspberries belong, are woody, *prickly, or bristly* shrubs with 5-petaled white flowers and juicy berries. There are perhaps 200 species in our area, and to separate them requires the expertise of the specialist. Many are described and illustrated in *A Field Guide to Trees and Shrubs* by George Petrides.

COMMON STRAWBERRY
Rose Family

Everyone knows the cultivated strawberry, but not everyone recognizes the *3-part leaf* of the wild kind until the smallish fruits appear. The small, round-petaled, white flowers are in a cluster on a separate 3- to 6-inch stalk, *no taller* than the leaves. Look for the flowers in open places from late April to June. The **Wood Strawberry** (not shown), an alien species, has flowers that are usually held *above* the leaves.

COMMON CHICKWEED
Pink Family

The little Chickweed, another import from Europe, invades our gardens, roadsides, and waste places. It is only a few inches high, and the split petals of its tiny, starlike blossoms are *shorter* than the sepals. The short, ovate leaves are on *thin stalks*, unlike those of the Star Chickweed (below).

STAR CHICKWEED
Pink Family

Larger than the Common Chickweed, this modest flower has sepals that are *shorter than* its split petals. Its leaves are *larger* and *usually not stalked*. This chickweed is a native plant, not an alien. Look for it in woodlands from Illinois and New Jersey south. It blooms in spring from March to May, whereas the Common Chickweed may be found in flower much of the year.

BRAMBLE
(BLACKBERRY)

COMMON
STRAWBERRY

COMMON
CHICKWEED

STAR CHICKWEED

DAME'S ROCKET
Mustard Family

This pretty garden escape, originally from Europe, resembles the Garden Phlox (see p. 85), but has *4 petals*, not 5. This, and the long, upward-pointing seedpods, tell us it belongs to the mustard family. Blooming mostly in May and June, before the Garden (Fall) Phlox comes into flower, Dame's Rocket can be pink, purple, or white. It decorates the shaded roadsides and wood edges of southern Canada, the northern U.S., and southward in the Appalachian uplands to Georgia.

TALL CINQUEFOIL
Rose Family

Most cinquefoils are yellow with leaves that are divided into 5 leaflets, as their family name suggests. However, this one is *white or creamy*, with 7 to 11 leaflets that are downy beneath. The *clammy, brownish hairs* on the stem also separate this species from other cinquefoils that are superficially similar (see p. 69). Tall Cinquefoil, standing 1 to 3 feet high, blooms from June to August, in the rocky soil of dry woods across southern Canada and the northern tier of states.

SWEET EVERLASTING
Daisy Family

Everlastings have *small, globular flower-heads* clustered at the tops of their pale, woolly stems. The Sweet Everlasting is not as attractive as the Pearly Everlasting (p. 25) because the *bracts* that enclose the staminate (male) flowers at the center *do not expand* until the plant is in seed. There are many kinds of everlastings that remain a puzzle even to professional botanists. Those with a rosette of basal leaves are usually called "pussytoes." Most species prefer dry soil.

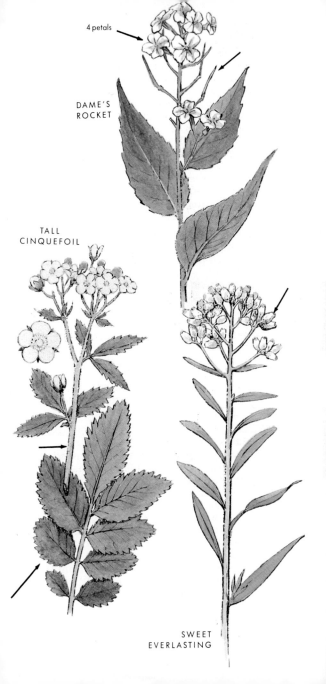

4 petals

DAME'S
ROCKET

TALL
CINQUEFOIL

SWEET
EVERLASTING

YARROW
Daisy Family

The tight, *flat-topped, white flower clusters* of this roadside plant are sometimes confused with the Wild Carrot or Queen Anne's Lace. Note, however, the soft, aromatic, highly dissected, *fernlike leaves,* quite unlike the *branched* (but also fernlike) leaves of the Wild Carrot (p. 27). Although usually white, Yarrow may sometimes be rose-pink, a form that is often transplanted to the garden. Yarrow is another of the many aliens that now grace the roadsides and field edges throughout much of eastern and central North America. It stands 1 to 3 feet tall.

PEARLY EVERLASTING
Rose Family

This pallid plant is more showy than the Sweet Everlasting (p. 22) because its dry, petal-like *white bracts spread a bit* to expose the yellow staminate center (male flowers). The pistillate (female) flowers are on separate plants. The stem is cottony, with *downy hairs.* The leaves are linear; gray-green above, woolly-white beneath. Like the other everlastings, this one is variable—a botanist's puzzle. It prefers dry soil and pastures across Canada, the northern U.S., and southward in the mountains to North Carolina.

BONESET
Daisy Family

Although this hairy plant is flat-topped, rather like Yarrow and Wild Carrot, it has very different leaves. Long, pointed, wrinkled, and hairy, the leaves are arranged in pairs that *unite around the stem.* Boneset prefers low wet ground, damp thickets, and swamps, where it comes into bloom in late summer at about the same time as its purplish relative, the Spotted Joe-Pye-weed (p. 90). Tea brewed from the dried leaves of Boneset is regarded as a good laxative.

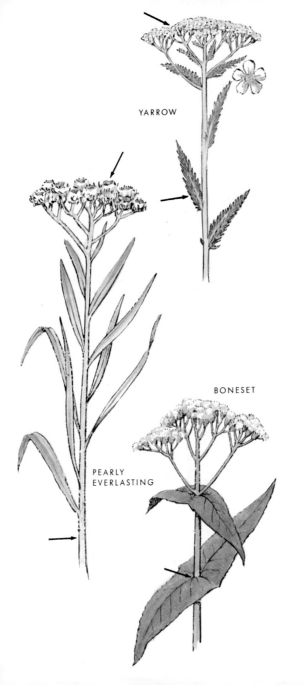

YARROW

PEARLY
EVERLASTING

BONESET

COW-PARSNIP
Parsley Family

This huge, woolly relative of the Wild Carrot (below) stands 4 to 8 or even 10 feet tall. It is a conspicuous plant on moist slopes across Canada and the border states and southward locally in the Appalachians. The ridged stem may be 2 inches thick at the base and the great umbel of rank-smelling white flowers may have a span of 8 inches. The leaves, often a foot long, are divided into *3 mapleleaf-like segments.* An *inflated sheath* joins each leaf stalk to the main stem. Summertime—June to August—is the time of bloom. A similar large species, **Angelica** (not shown), has a smooth, *dark purple stem* and *smaller leaves.*

WILD CARROT, QUEEN ANNE'S LACE
Parsley Family

The *flat clusters* of innumerable small white flowers that form an intricate, lace-like pattern give this abundant plant its popular name of Queen Anne's Lace. After their bloom is past, the old umbels curl to form a *cuplike "birds' nest;"* this has given rise to another popular name. The leaves, savored by caterpillars of the Black Swallowtail butterfly, are finely cut, like those of a number of similar plants in the parsley or carrot family. A successful invader from the Old World, the Wild Carrot, standing 2 to 3 feet tall, lines the roadsides in summer and literally turns some dry fields quite white with its lacy banners.

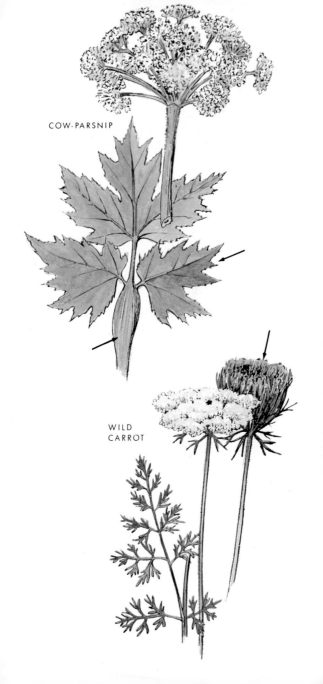

COW-PARSNIP

WILD CARROT

ALSIKE CLOVER
Pea Family

The clovers, with their round heads of
small, pea-like blossoms and their 3-parted
leaves, are familiar to everyone. There are
several white clovers. This clover, ranging
from creamy white to pink, *does not*
exhibit the pale chevrons on its leaflets as
does the White Clover (next). Its leaves and
flowers *spring from branching stems*
above the ground, not from subsurface
runners. This is another alien plant that
has established itself in fields and roadsides
throughout our area, where it blooms
during the summer months. **Buffalo Clover**
(not shown), a native of dry woods and
prairies in the lower Midwest, has leaflets
that are somewhat *heart-shaped* or *slightly
notched*. The flowers are white or white
and red.

WHITE CLOVER
Pea Family

This clover has a *pale triangular chevron*
on each leaf. The flowers and leaflets are on
separate stalks, rising 4 to 8 inches from
creeping runners just below the surface
of the ground. Like the Alsike Clover, this
familiar alien from the Old World has
become well established along our roadsides,
field edges, and even on our lawns. The
flowers, which may be white or tinged with
pink, bloom from May to October.

WHITE SWEET-CLOVER
Pea Family

The 3-parted leaves and the pea-like shape
of the tiny florets suggest that this plant
is a clover, but the flowers are arranged in
slim, tapering clusters. Unlike the ground-
hugging clovers, this plant rises in a
flimsy, spindly manner to a height of 2 to 8
feet. Although of alien origin, it is now
abundant along roadsides and field edges
throughout our area, blooming from May
to October. See also Yellow Sweet-clover
(p. 70).

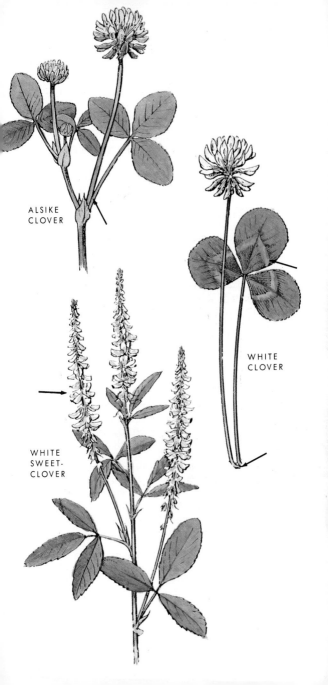

ALSIKE
CLOVER

WHITE
CLOVER

WHITE
SWEET-
CLOVER

SILVER-ROD
Daisy Family

Of the many kinds of goldenrods, this is the only *white* one. It is wandlike, standing 1 to 3 feet tall. Its small composite flowers are arranged in little clusters along the upper part of the hairy, grayish stem. Silver-rod blooms from July to October in open dry woodlands and on open slopes.

WHITE LETTUCE, RATTLESNAKE-ROOT
Daisy Family

The rattlesnake-roots are tall, slender, weedy plants with *triangular or deeply lobed leaves;* they are extremely variable. When broken, the stems exude a milkweed-like juice. The bell-like flowers hang in *drooping clusters.* This species has *creamy white flowers,* often tinged with greenish or lilac. Like the yellow and blue species (see pp. 55 and 105), this wild lettuce blooms in early autumn. There are 10 species of rattlesnake-roots in our area, some reaching a height of 7 feet. They are much alike but can be separated using fine points to be found in technical botanies.

POKEWEED, POKE
Pokeweed Family

This tall, weedy, large-leaved plant grows to a height of 4 to 10 feet in damp thickets, clearings, and along roadsides. It is readily identified by its coarse *reddish stems* and, late in the season, by its long, drooping clusters of purple-black berries with *red stalks.* The greenish white "petals" of the small flowers are really sepals. The tempting-looking berries are poisonous and so is the carrotlike root.

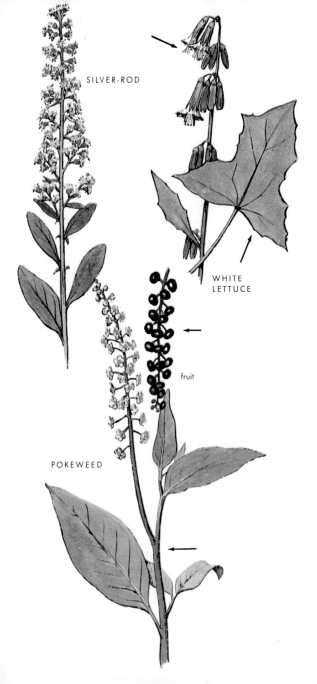

SILVER-ROD

WHITE
LETTUCE

fruit

POKEWEED

BOUNCING BET
Pink Family

Clusters of these *ragged-looking, scallop-tipped flowers* form roadside gardens from July to September. The flowers are *pink or whitish*, sometimes with double petals; the leaves and stems are smooth. Bouncing Bet is one of the many aliens from Europe that have taken over our roadsides and waste places. Call them weeds if you will, but they lend beauty to the otherwise drab and disturbed soils.

EVENING LYCHNIS, WHITE CAMPION
Pink Family

This introduction from Europe blooms at night, when its white flowers attract moths to perform the mystic rites of pollination. Each flower consists of 5 deeply cleft petals. Below it is an *inflated sac* or calyx, which is *sticky*, preventing ants from stealing the sweets. There are several other campions in our area, some native, some not. The Evening Lychnis favors waste places, where it blooms from June to September.

TURTLEHEAD
Snapdragon Family

Late summer, when the Cardinal-flower (p. 78) is in bloom by the streambanks and shady wet places, is the time to look for the Turtlehead. Its snapdragon-like flowers are set in a tight cluster at the tip of the stem. The turtle-like *upper lip arching over the lower lip* suggests the plant's name. The flowers are usually white, but may be tinged with pink. The broad leaves, arranged opposite each other along the stem, are coarsely toothed. An alien species, the **Red Turtlehead** (not shown), has been introduced locally in New England. A similar red species with narrower leaves is found in the interior and along the southern coastal plain.

BOUNCING BET

EVENING
LYCHNIS

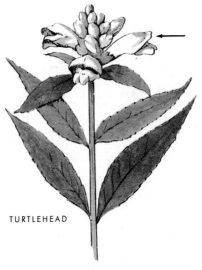

TURTLEHEAD

SHEPHERD'S PURSE
Mustard Family

This alien "weed" is most easily recognized by its small, flat, *heart-shaped seedpods*. The white flowers are tiny and the stem leaves are small and clasping, unlike the *dandelion-like leaves* at the base. It blooms from April to September in waste ground. The **Field Pennycress** (not shown), also an alien "weed" of waste ground, has much larger, *round* seedpods ("pennies"), each with a *deep notch* at the tip.

ENGLISH PLANTAIN
Plantain Family

This modest dooryard "weed" that thrives in waste places and along sterile roadsides is another alien, pre-adapted to survival under similar conditions in the Old World. This plantain has a grooved stalk from 9 to 20 inches tall, topped by a *short, bushy flowerhead* that extends beyond the *long, almost grasslike leaves.* The English Plantain blooms from April to November. A shorter, fleshier species with a *longer* flowerhead, the **Seaside Plantain** (not shown), grows along the outer coast, from New Jersey northward.

COMMON PLANTAIN
Plantain Family

This low dooryard "weed" often grows in the same places and under the same conditions as the English Plantain, but instead of being tall and slender it is relatively squat, with *broad, oval or spade-shaped leaves.* These are strongly ribbed and sprawl on troughlike stems. The flower stalk is *long and tight,* quite unlike the short, bushy flowerhead of the English Plantain. Both species are introductions from Europe, but do very well here under spartan conditions. Although these alien weeds seldom command our attention, they have become an important part of our urban flora.

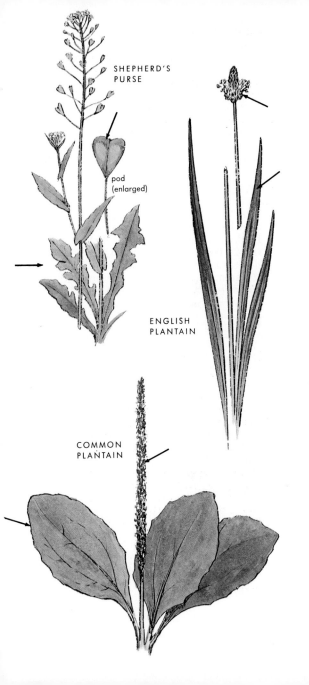

SHEPHERD'S PURSE

pod
(enlarged)

ENGLISH PLANTAIN

COMMON PLANTAIN

FALSE SOLOMON'S-SEAL
Lily Family

The oval, pointed leaves are spaced alternately along the reclining stem, which *terminates* in a *spirea-like cluster* of small, creamy white flowers. Solomon's-seal (p. 125) looks similar, but the *twinned flowers dangle* from the *leaf axils.* False Solomon's-seal blooms in the woods from May to July. The fruits—whitish berries speckled with brown—later become ruby-red.

THREE-LEAVED FALSE SOLOMON'S-SEAL
Lily Family

This little woodland plant of early summer may be confused with the Wild Lily-of-the-Valley (below), but usually has *3 leaves,* not 2. The small, *star-shaped* white flowers have 6 petals and alternate along the stem above the shiny, pointed leaves, which *taper* at the base and sheath the stem.

WILD LILY-OF-THE-VALLEY
Lily Family

Often confused with the Three-leaved False Solomon's-seal, the "Canada Mayflower" (as it is sometimes called) often forms large mats in cool woodlands. It can be recognized by the *2 heart-shaped leaves* that clasp the stem. Rarely it may have 3; then examine the tiny white flowers bunched in a tight cluster. These have *4 petals,* not 6. The berries, white with spots, later turn pale red.

EARLY MEADOW-RUE
Buttercup Family

Note the *drooping* flowers that lack petals. The male flowers, growing separately from the female (pistillate) flowers, have numerous yellow stamens protruding from greenish white, petal-like sepals. The long-stalked leaves are divided into roundish leaflets. This flimsy woodland plant blooms *early* in the year (April to May).

FALSE
SOLOMON'S-SEAL

6 petals

THREE-LEAVED
FALSE
SOLOMON'S
SEAL

6 petals

4 petals

EARLY
MEADOW-RUE

WILD LILY-OF-THE-VALLEY

OX-EYE DAISY
Daisy Family

What would our roadsides and waste places be without the escapes and imports from the Old World? Some we call "weeds" and regard with contempt; others, like the white Ox-eye Daisy, are much cherished. Even the plebeian Dandelion is really very handsome, prettier than most of its close relatives, our native hawkweeds. The Daisy's yellow, *buttonlike disk, flattened* in the center, contains the true flowers—the white "petals" are really rays. Daisies bloom all summer in our fields and roadsides. Flowers of the Daisy Family are also called "composites."

FEVERFEW
Daisy Family

This bushy plant, with its numerous small, daisylike flowers, has *relatively larger* yellow buttons than the Ox-eye Daisy and *much stubbier* white rays. It is a roadside escape, originally planted as a garden flower.

MAYWEED
Daisy Family

This, another small, daisylike plant, is recognized by its *finely cut,* yarrow-like leaves. The **Wild Chamomile** (not shown) is still another daisylike "weed." Its leaves are *more threadlike* than those of the Mayweed. Both plants came from Europe and have found our roadsides and waste places congenial. They bloom throughout the summer.

DAISY FLEABANE
Daisy Family

Unlike the asters, all of which bloom in late summer or fall, this white asterlike flower blooms in the *spring,* as well as in the months that follow. Its *petal-like rays* are *numerous* (40 to 70). The stems are *hairy* and the leaves are strongly toothed. This plant is common in field edges, along roadsides, and in wastelands throughout our area.

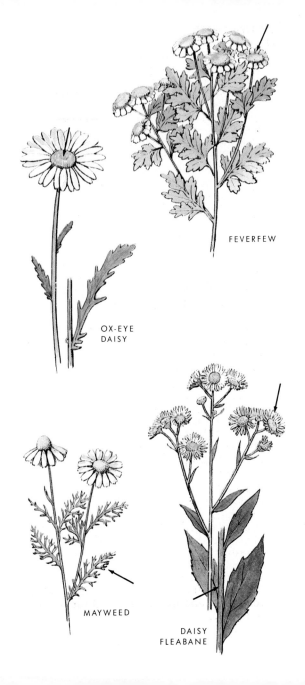

FEVERFEW

OX-EYE
DAISY

MAYWEED

DAISY
FLEABANE

SMALL WHITE ASTER
Daisy Family

Scores, even hundreds, of *small white flowers crowd the smooth purple stems* of this aster, giving it a lace-like look. The slender leaves have *small leaflets in the axils,* as shown in the drawing opposite. This aster, one of the many species of white asters, comes into bloom from August to October in fields and meadows from Michigan, southern Ontario, and southern Maine southward. Fourteen kinds of white asters are shown in *A Field Guide to Wildflowers.*

FLAT-TOPPED WHITE ASTER
Daisy Family

This white aster, with its distinctive *flat-topped clusters,* has relatively few rays (2 to 15). The yellow disk at the center turns *purplish* with age. The lance-shaped leaves are *toothless.* This is an abundant species, growing from 2 to 7 feet tall in thickets and woodland edges, as well as along brushy roadsides. It is widespread in eastern Canada and the northeastern states, extending southward in the cooler Appalachians.

WHITE WOOD ASTER
Daisy Family

This low white aster of the open woods is readily identified by its *stalked, heart-shaped leaves.* The clusters of flowers tend to be flat-topped, but the heart-shaped leaves easily separate this aster from the much taller Flat-topped Aster, described above. The White Wood Aster blooms from July to October, from Ohio to southern New England and southward in the woodlands of the Appalachians to Georgia. See purple asters on p. 102.

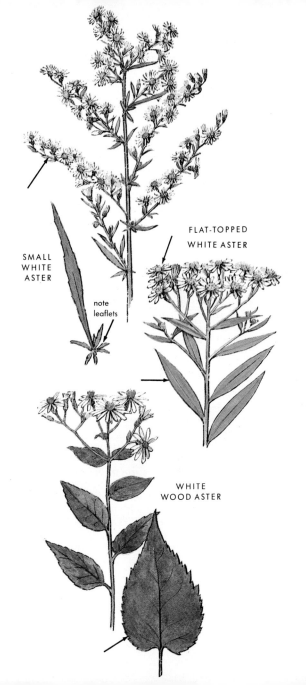

SMALL
WHITE
ASTER

note
leaflets

FLAT-TOPPED
WHITE ASTER

WHITE
WOOD ASTER

BULLHEAD-LILY
Water-lily Family

This is the familiar yellow water-lily of the Northeast, where its *platterlike leaves float* on the quiet waters of ponds and sluggish rivers. The fleshy, globular, yellow "petals" are actually sepals. The real petals are stamenlike and are quite concealed. There is a disklike stigma in the center. The broad green leaves are deeply notched at the point where they are joined to the immersed stem. The Bullhead-lily blooms from May to September across Canada and the northern states. Southward it is replaced by the **Spatterdock** (not shown), which looks very similar but usually holds its leaves above the water.

MARSH-MARIGOLD, COWSLIP
Buttercup Family

Shaped like huge buttercups, the 1- to 1½-inch flowers grace swamps and brooksides in spring, from April to June. The glossy, *roundish or kidney-shaped leaves* and the thick, succulent stems make good eating when stewed as greens, especially early in the season before they become too coarse. They have a sweeter taste than dandelion greens, which are rather bitter.

YELLOW IRIS
Iris Family

This alien relative of the Blue Flag (p. 106) is the only *yellow* iris likely to be found growing wild. Although there are other kinds of yellow irises in our gardens, this European species is the only one that has escaped to grace some of our stream-sides and wetlands. Although it has become established widely, it is rather spotty in distribution. Blooming from May to July, it is conspicuous along the Potomac River near Washington, D.C. and along some of the other rivers on the Atlantic Seaboard.

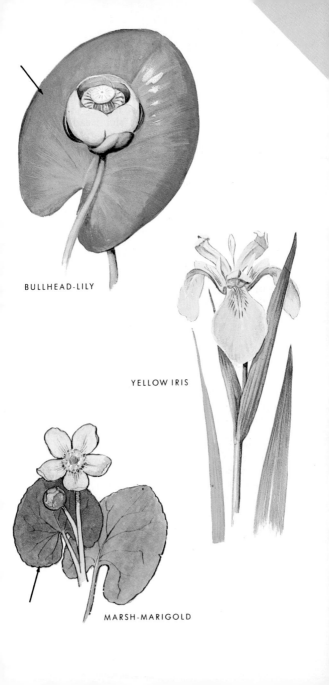

BULLHEAD-LILY

YELLOW IRIS

MARSH-MARIGOLD

TROUT-LILY, ADDER'S-TONGUE
Lily Family

This little yellow lily, standing only 4 to 10 inches high, is a springtime favorite of the woods-walker. The *reflexed yellow petals* are often purplish beneath and the two large basal leaves are heavily *mottled with brown*. The time of bloom is from March to May in woodlands from Minnesota, Ontario, and Nova Scotia southward. Similar white forms or species occur elsewhere in our country.

CLINTONIA
Lily Family

Two or three *yellowish green bells* rise on a leafless stalk above 2 or 3 broad, shining basal leaves; in due time the flowers are replaced by deep blue berries. This modest little lily blooms from May to July in cool woods and on the open slopes of mountains of Canada and the adjacent northern states, extending southward in the mountains to Georgia. A similar species, the **White Clintonia** (not shown), is found from eastern Ohio and western New York southward in the Appalachian Mountains.

YELLOW LADY'S-SLIPPER
Orchid Family

The *saclike "slipper"* and the *spirally twisted brown petals* of this lovely yellow orchid are distinctive. Bogs, wet woods, and shady swamps form the environment of this rather scarce flower. It varies in size, from the smaller form shown here to the one known as the **Large Yellow Lady's-slipper.** In one form or another, this very special flower blooms from May to July from Quebec and Newfoundland south locally to the mountains of Georgia. It is an endangered species in some localities. Admire it, but do not pick it. See the Pink Lady's-slipper and Showy Lady's-slipper on p. 77.

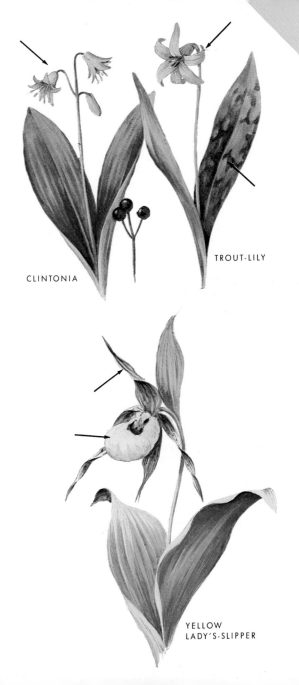

CLINTONIA

TROUT-LILY

YELLOW
LADY'S-SLIPPER

SUNDROPS
Evening-primrose Family

Unlike their close relatives, the evening-primroses, sundrops are day-bloomers. The 4 yellow petals, *orange stamens,* and strongly ribbed seedpods are distinctive. They also have the X-shaped stigma typical of the family. The leaves are *plain-edged,* unlike the rougher leaves of the Common Evening-primrose (below). There are several similar species of sundrops. The sunny blossoms can be found in meadows and fields from June to August.

COMMON EVENING-PRIMROSE
Evening-primrose Family

There are at least 15 kinds of evening-primroses in our area and some are difficult to identify. They can be divided into two groups: evening-primroses, which open their yellow flowers toward evening and wilt next day, and sundrops, which prefer the sunshine. The Common Evening-primrose, shown here, is typical of the group, which always has *4 petals,* an *X-shaped stigma* in the center of the flower, and *reflexed sepals.* This, the best-known member of the family, is *leafy,* branched, and rough-hairy. It often has reddish stems. A common roadside plant, it blooms from June to September in dry or sandy soil.

DOWNY FALSE FOXGLOVE
Snapdragon Family

False foxgloves have *bell-shaped, golden flowers* with 5 widely spread lobes or "petals." The several kinds are similar except for their leaves. This one has deeply lobed, *downy leaves* and downy stems. Believed to be parasitic on oaks, false foxgloves bloom in late summer in dry open woods. **Smooth False Foxglove** (not shown) is *smooth,* with leaves that are less deeply cut. **Fern-leaved False Foxglove** (not shown) has lacy, *fernlike* leaves.

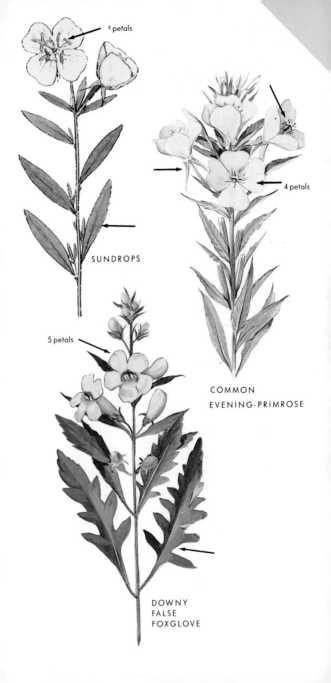

4 petals

SUNDROPS

4 petals

COMMON
EVENING-PRIMROSE

5 petals

DOWNY
FALSE
FOXGLOVE

MOTH MULLEIN
Snapdragon Family

This pretty alien is as delicate and slender as its relative the Common Mullein (below) is sturdy. This mullein's sparse, round-petaled flowers may be yellow or white and are tinged with dull purplish on the back. The points to look for are the scant foliage, the *buttonlike buds*, the *orange anthers*, and the *purplish "beards"* on the stamens. Moth Mullein blooms from June to September along road shoulders and in dry fields and waste places. The name "Moth Mullein" comes from its fuzzy stamens, which suggest the antennae of a moth.

BUTTER-AND-EGGS, TOADFLAX
Snapdragon Family

During the summer months, from June to October, this attractive alien pleases the eye along roadsides, and in dry fields and waste places that would otherwise be quite drab. The clublike *spikes of snapdragonlike flowers* are yellow with *orange palates* and thin, drooping spurs. Numerous small, narrow leaves climb the stem.

COMMON MULLEIN
Snapdragon Family

It is impossible not to notice this sturdy plant that has come to us from the other side of the Atlantic. Standing at least 2 feet tall, and sometimes as tall as 6 feet, it is topped with a *clublike flowerhead.* The flowers start blossoming at the bottom of the long bud cluster and continue opening toward the top as the days go by. The large, *flannel-textured leaves* flow into the stem. The Common Mullein grows along roadsides and in poor soil nearly throughout our area. A similar alien, the **Clasping-leaved Mullein** (not shown), has a more *open* flowerhead. Its woolly leaves do not flow into the stem.

BUTTER-AND-EGGS

MOTH
MULLEIN

COMMON
MULLEIN

COMMON ST. JOHNSWORT
St. Johnswort Family
This alien plant, which does so well along roadsides, weedy fields, and in waste places, displays its clusters of yellow flowers all summer long. The 5-petaled yellow flowers have a *cluster of bushy stamens* in the center and *black dots on the margins* of the petals. Upon examination the rather small, paired leaves show translucent dots. There are a number of other St. Johnsworts (not shown), most of them native, varying in size from the **Great St. Johnswort**, with flowers measuring 2 to 3 inches across, to the **Dwarf St. Johnswort**, with blossoms less than one-half inch across.

YELLOW LOOSESTRIFE, SWAMP CANDLES
Primrose Family
In midsummer a *slender spike* of small, starlike, yellow flowers comes into bloom in swampy places and along grassy shores. Note particularly the *circle of red spots* on the petals. The leaves ascend the stem in pairs. This species, one of several yellow-flowered loosestrifes, grows widely in wet places throughout our area. The **Garden Loosestrife** (not shown) sometimes escapes cultivation and goes wild. It is a coarser, bushier, densely downy plant. Its flowers are in a tall, branched cluster in the upper leaf axils.

WHORLED LOOSESTRIFE
Primrose Family
This delicate plant grows in open woods, along forest edges, and on shores. Its leaves are arranged in *whorls of 4*. From the base of each leaf a small, 5-petaled yellow flower is carried on a threadlike stem. Each flower is dotted around the center with *red*. This is but one of many loosestrifes belonging to the primrose family. The Purple Loosestrife on p. 83 belongs to the loosestrife family.

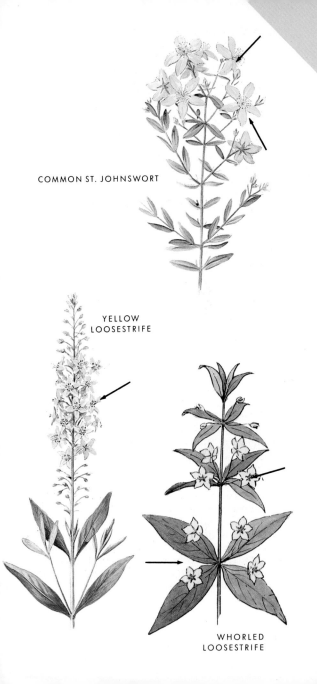

COMMON ST. JOHNSWORT

YELLOW
LOOSESTRIFE

WHORLED
LOOSESTRIFE

COMMON DANDELION
Daisy Family

Who does not know the Dandelion? As children playing on the lawn we have all grown up with Dandelions. Some home-owners weed them out so as to give a pooltable-like look to their lawns; others leave them alone and regard them as welcome harbingers of spring, like the Robins. There is no mistaking the *jagged leaves*, the *reflexed sepals* below the flowerhead, the *hollow stem* that oozes a milky juice when broken, and the *round, fluffy seedballs*. This alien from the Old World blooms all summer long throughout our land.

YELLOW GOATS-BEARD
Daisy Family

Much more slender than the lowly Dande-lion, the Yellow Goats-beard may be recog-nized by the *grasslike leaves* that embrace its stem, and the *long green bracts* that support the flower, which closes at midday. The bracts of the ordinary Dandelion are bent downward. Both plants exude a milky juice when their stems are broken. This successful alien finds many of our roadsides and field edges to its liking. Its globular puffballs of seeds are much like those of the Dandelion but *larger*, and on *longer stalks*. A closely related species known as the **Oyster Plant** (not shown) has reddish flowers; the two often hybridize.

COMMON SOW-THISTLE
Daisy Family

Like tall, *prickly* Dandelions, Sow-thistles are to be found in waste places and along field edges and roadsides. In addition to the Common Sow-thistle, shown here, there is the **Field Sow-thistle,** with *weaker spines*, and the **Spiny Sow-thistle,** with big, *earlike lobes* that clasp the stem. All are aliens from Europe, as is their better-known relative, the Dandelion.

COMMON
DANDELION

YELLOW
GOATS-BEARD

COMMON
SOW-THISTLE

WILD LETTUCE
Daisy Family

The *loose clusters* of small, pale, dandelion-like flowers and, to a certain extent, the *shape of the leaves,* show the relationship of the wild lettuces to the dandelions and hawkweeds, but Wild Lettuce towers over them all, standing *4 to 10 feet tall.* Its lower leaves may be as much as 10 inches long. Whereas this species is yellow, there are similar white and blue lettuces (see pp. 31 and 105). Wild Lettuce blooms in late summer, from July to September, along brushy roadsides and in clearings throughout most of our area.

CANADA HAWKWEED
Daisy Family

Like the various other hawkweeds (not shown here), this plant has a loose terminal cluster of small, dandelion-like flowers, but the leaves that crowd the stem are *coarsely toothed.* Found along wood edges and roadside thickets, Canada Hawkweed blooms in late summer from Canada south to the Great Lakes states and New Jersey. The **Hairy Hawkweed** (not shown) is more slender, with several large, *hairy* leaves on the lower half of the stem and *none higher up.*

KING DEVIL
Daisy Family

The various kinds of hawkweeds look like miniature dandelions, to which they are related. This is a hairy species; its *stems and bracts* are *bristly* with *blackish hairs.* It blooms during the summer months (May to August) in the fields and roadsides of eastern Canada, the northeastern U.S., and southward in the mountains. Another alien, the **Orange Hawkweed** (not shown), sometimes called "Devil's Paintbrush," looks like a deep orange version of King Devil. The two often grow in the same fields.

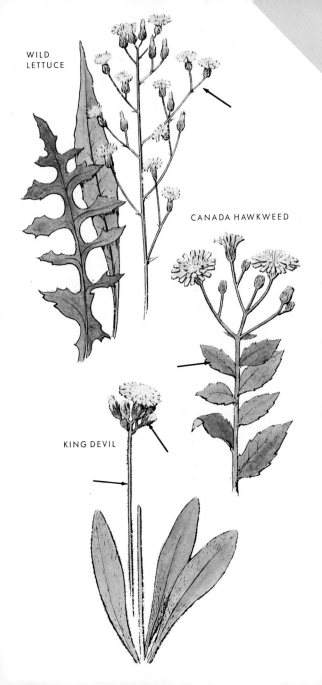

WILD LETTUCE

CANADA HAWKWEED

KING DEVIL

COMMON SUNFLOWER
Daisy Family

This is a smaller wild edition of the cultivated Sunflower (which may bear flowers 10 inches across). The rough, toothed, *heart-shaped or spade-shaped leaves* are carried on slender stalks. Standing 3 to 12 feet tall, the Common Sunflower is at home in the prairies and fields of the Midwest, but has become established locally in the East, especially along roadsides. There are a number of kinds of other wild sunflowers, best identified by their leaf structure and arrangement (see *A Field Guide to Wildflowers*).

BLACK-EYED SUSAN
Daisy Family

In this showy composite, each daisylike flower, with its numerous *golden-yellow rays* and *chocolate button*, is carried singly on a slender *bristly* stalk. The leaves are also bristly or hairy. Although the Black-eyed Susan now grows in fields and open woods nearly throughout our area, it apparently was an early invader from the Midwest, reaching the Eastern Seaboard states among seeds of clover. The blooming season is from June to October. The **Thin-leaved Coneflower** (not shown) has smaller, more numerous flowers with fewer (8–10) rays. Its lower leaves have *3 lobes*.

GREEN-HEADED CONEFLOWER
Daisy Family

This handsome, daisylike flower stands 3 to 10 feet tall. It is closely related to the familiar Black-eyed Susan, but the protruding central button or disk is *green*, not chocolate-brown. The yellow rays are *reflexed (bent downward)* and the leaves are *deeply cut* into 3 to 5 parts. The Green-headed Coneflower blooms from July to September, in moist rich ground from southern Canada southward.

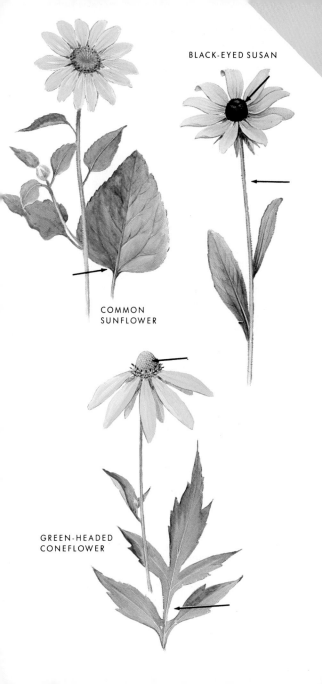

BLACK-EYED SUSAN

COMMON
SUNFLOWER

GREEN-HEADED
CONEFLOWER

TICKSEED-SUNFLOWER
Daisy Family

There are a number of kinds of tickseeds, or "sticktights." Anyone who has picked the *flat, pronged seeds* from their stockings or trousers knows these bothersome plants. The Tickseed-sunflower, shown here, is one of the showier members of this group (genus *Bidens*). It blooms in late summer and early fall, in wet meadows and swampy spots from Minnesota, the Great Lakes, and Maine southward. Some species of the genus have no petal-like rays but make themselves known by their tenacious seeds, which have given them the name "beggar-ticks."

LANCE-LEAVED COREOPSIS
Daisy Family

This yellow, daisylike flower has 8 petal-like rays. Each ray is *scalloped, with 4 lobes* at its tip. The central button or disk is *yellow*, not chocolate-brown as in the Black-eyed Susan and similar species. The slender, lance-shaped leaves often have *2 basal prongs*. Blooming in early summer in poor soil, frequently by the roadside, it is basically a flower of the Midwest, from Wisconsin, Michigan and Ontario south, but it has also established itself locally in the Northeast, where originally it may have been an escape from gardens.

WOODLAND SUNFLOWER
Daisy Family

There are many kinds of wild sunflowers, all much smaller than the common Sunflower of the garden and more suggestive of yellow daisies. This one can be recognized by its *tapering leaves*, which are very rough above and hairy below. Standing 2 to 6½ feet, it blooms from July to October in open woods and dry thickets from southern Canada and Maine southward.

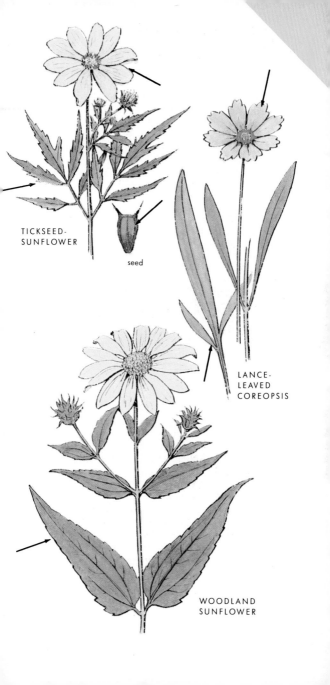

TICKSEED-
SUNFLOWER

seed

LANCE-
LEAVED
COREOPSIS

WOODLAND
SUNFLOWER

EARLY GOLDENROD
Daisy Family

Goldenrods can be confusing; all are yellow except for the Silver-rod (p. 30). Their flower clusters vary in form from plumelike to clublike, wandlike, wide-spreading, or flat-topped. This is one of the tapering plumed species. Note the *tiny, winglike leaflets* in the axils of the *slim, toothless* upper leaves. This goldenrod blooms from July to September in the dry soil of roadsides, rocky banks, and open woods, from southern Canada to the central states and southward to Georgia in the hilly country to Georgia.

CANADA GOLDENROD
Daisy Family

There are many kinds of goldenrods in our area; 30 are shown in *A Field Guide to Wildflowers of Northeastern and North-central North America.* Some look much alike except for the shape, dentition, veining, and arrangement of the leaves. For this reason the differences are easier to see in line drawings. Canada Goldenrod, with its graceful plume and *sharply toothed leaves crowded* along the stem, is perhaps the most familiar species. It blooms from July to September along roadsides, in fields, and in clearings.

SEASIDE GOLDENROD
Daisy Family

Along the coast, in the dunes, above the high-tide line on the beaches, and at the edge of the salt marsh, this showy goldenrod blooms from August to November, playing host to migrating Monarch butterflies. The smooth, stout stem and *slim, toothless leaves* have a *fleshy texture.* It varies in shape, and even hybridizes with the Rough-stemmed Goldenrod, which has toothed leaves. This virile composite flourishes from the Gulf of St. Lawrence to the southern states, where it is less showy.

EARLY
GOLDENROD

CANADA
GOLDENROD

SEASIDE
GOLDENROD

LANCE-LEAVED GOLDENROD
Daisy Family

This is the common *flat-topped* goldenrod. The *slender, willowlike leaves* have rough, untoothed edges and 3 to 5 *parallel nerves* (unbranched veins). Like the next species, it is fragrant. Blooming as early as July and sometimes lasting till October, it favors wet thickets, damp roadsides, and banks of streams.

BLUE-STEMMED GOLDENROD
Daisy Family

This goldenrod, which blooms from August to October in woodlands and thickets, is easy to tell because the *well-spaced flower tufts* are in the *axils* of the smooth, slender leaves, where they join the *purplish stem.*

ELM-LEAVED GOLDENROD
Daisy Family

The *spreading flower clusters* of this goldenrod suggest the graceful branches of an elm. It can be confused with the **Rough-leaved Goldenrod** (not shown), but the latter has a sharply *4-angled stem* and *much larger lower leaves* that may be more than 12 inches long. Whereas the Elm-leaved Goldenrod prefers dry woodlands and thickets, the Rough-leaved Goldenrod favors swamps, bogs, and wet meadows.

SLENDER FRAGRANT GOLDENROD
Daisy Family

This flat-topped goldenrod is similar to the previous species but its leaves are smoother and more delicately cut. The grasslike leaves have *only one nerve* (not 3) and are minutely dotted. The plant is very fragrant, especially when crushed. Favoring sandy soil and the edges of salt marshes, mainly near the coast, it thrives from Nova Scotia and Maine to Florida. A similar species is found near the southern shores of Lake Michigan and Lake Erie.

LANCE-LEAVED GOLDENROD

BLUE-STEMMED GOLDENROD

ELM-LEAVED GOLDENROD

SLENDER FRAGRANT GOLDENROD

SMOOTH YELLOW VIOLET
Violet Family

Violets suggest tiny pansies and come in various shades of white, yellow, blue, and violet. There are several kinds of yellow violets. This one may be recognized by its *smooth stems* and its broadly *heart-shaped basal leaves*, as well as by the *additional leaves* on the flower stem. The spring months, April to June, bring these shy flowers into bloom in the meadows and low woods. The **Downy Yellow Violet** (not shown) has a *downy* stem and leaves. It usually lacks the basal leaves of the Smooth Yellow Violet.

COMMON BUTTERCUP
Buttercup Family

There are many kinds of buttercups, some native, others alien. A dozen kinds are shown in the *Field Guide to Wildflowers*. This alien species, familiar to everyone, serves as the prototype. It is *erect*, branching, and hairy. The petals overlap and the basal leaves are *deeply divided* into 5 to 7 segments. Buttercups bloom from May to September in fields and meadows. The **Creeping Buttercup** (not shown), another widespread alien, can be recognized by its *creeping runners* and the *pale blotches* on its leaves.

CELANDINE
Poppy Family

Although the Celandine looks superficially like a buttercup, it belongs to the poppy family. Note that it has *only 4 petals*, not 5, and a somewhat different *leaf shape*. An alien, it has established itself about towns and moist wood edges throughout much of our area, blooming from March to May. The **Celandine-poppy** or **Wood-poppy** (not shown), is a similar native species, found mainly west of the Appalachians. Its flowers are larger and the stem leaves are arranged *in pairs*.

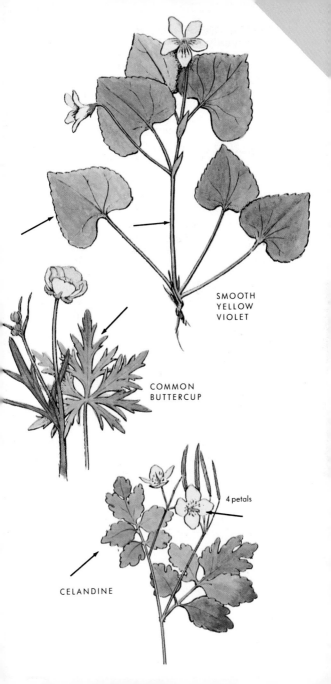

SMOOTH
YELLOW
VIOLET

COMMON
BUTTERCUP

CELANDINE

4 petals

COMMON TANSY
Daisy Family

Along roadsides during the latter part of summer, weedlike patches of this alien greet the traveler. The plants have flat-topped clusters of *golden buttons*, each of which looks like the central disk of a daisy minus the adorning white rays. The *fernlike leaves* have a strong scent.

GOLDEN ALEXANDERS
Parsley Family

This member of the parsley family has a *bright yellow umbel*, whereas the majority (but not all) of the others in this large family, such as the Wild Carrot (p. 26), are white. This golden flower blooms in wet thickets and swamps from April to early June, when the warblers and other migrants are pouring through. Its leaves are divided into *3 stalked leaflets* that are *subdivided* into 3 or more parts. The alien **Wild Parsnip** (not shown) is also yellow. The umbel is *more open* and the stout stem is *deeply grooved*.

BLACK MUSTARD
Mustard Family

There are many kinds of mustards; most have terminal clusters of small, 4-petaled yellow flowers and deeply lobed lower leaves. The seedpods are erect or nearly so, ending in a slender beak. Black Mustard has *seedpods* that *hug the stem*. The lower leaves are *coarsely lobed and bristly*; the upper leaves *slender and hairless*. This alien "weed" blooms in waste places and fields from June to October.

FIELD MUSTARD
Mustard Family

This alien has found a niche on our side of the Atlantic, mainly in open fields. The *earlike lobes* of the smaller leaves of this smooth, gray-green plant *clasp the stem*. The erect seedpods do *not* hug the stem as closely as those of the Black Mustard.

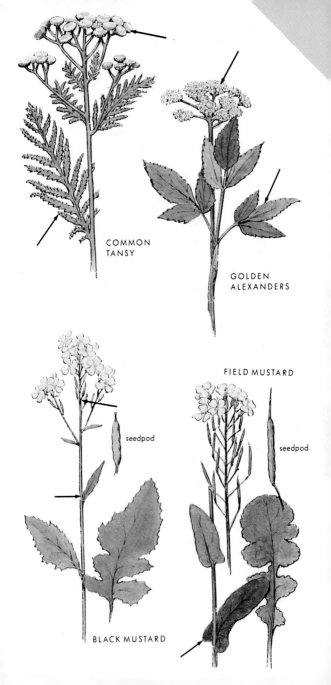

COMMON
TANSY

GOLDEN
ALEXANDERS

FIELD MUSTARD

seedpod

seedpod

BLACK MUSTARD

YELLOW WOOD-SORREL
Wood-sorrel Family
Wood-sorrels come in several colors—yellow, white, or lavender (see pp. 17 and 87). Each cloverlike or shamrocklike leaf is divided into 3 inverted heart-shaped leaflets. This yellow species is known by the *sharp angle* formed by the erect seedpods and their stalks. The alien **Creeping Wood-sorrel** (not shown) has *creeping stems.* The **Large Yellow Wood-sorrel** (not shown) has larger flowers and *larger leaves* which often have purple margins.

INDIAN STRAWBERRY
Rose Family
Although superficially like a strawberry, the fruit is inedible. This alien species flowers in moist waste ground from April to July. The **Barren Strawberry** (not shown), a native, *lacks runners.* Its leaves are *blunt,* not pointed, and it *does not produce berries.*

ROUGH-FRUITED CINQUEFOIL
Rose Family
Cinquefoil (5-leaf) is an appropriate name for most of the plants in this genus, but some have leaves that are subdivided into 7 or more leaflets. This species, an alien, is erect, hairy, and very leafy, with many branches. Although the *leaflets* are *usually in 5's,* there *may be 7.* The *pale* yellow flowers bloom from June to August in waste fields and along roadsides.

COMMON CINQUEFOIL
Rose Family
Cinquefoils suggest yellow-flowered wild strawberries, but most kinds have 5-parted leaves. This native species has *prostrate stems* that trail on the ground and root at the nodes. The flowers and leaves rise from the runners on separate stalks. This demure plant blooms in fields and dry woods from April to June.

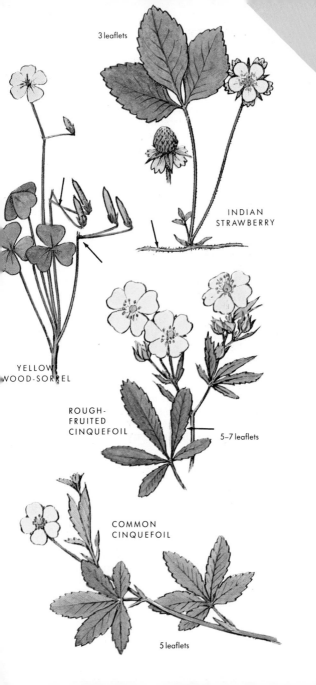

3 leaflets

INDIAN
STRAWBERRY

YELLOW
WOOD-SORREL

ROUGH-
FRUITED
CINQUEFOIL

5–7 leaflets

COMMON
CINQUEFOIL

5 leaflets

YELLOW SWEET-CLOVER
Pea Family

Along the open roadsides a spindly plant, 2 to 5 feet tall, displays *tapering spikes* of small, yellow, pea-like flowers during the summer months. It gives off a sweet odor when crushed. A similar plant, the **White Sweet-clover,** is shown on p. 29. Both sweet-clovers are alien plants, introduced from the Old World.

GORSE, FURZE
Pea Family

Although the yellow pea-like flowers look much like those of its fellow alien, the Broom (below), its branches do not. The dense tangle of leafless twigs armed with *sharp spines* make this a formidable shrub. An escape from cultivation, it grows locally in sandy soil along the coast from southeastern Massachusetts to Virginia.

PARTRIDGE-PEA, LARGE SENSITIVE-PLANT
Pea Family

The *finely cut compound leaves* of this low plant of sandy soil are somewhat sensitive to the touch. Unlike the related **Wild Sienna** (not shown), which has larger leaves but smaller flowers, it puts most of its energy into its rather large flowers. Note the *drooping dark anthers* that overhang the lower of the 5 petals. A smaller species, the **Wild Sensitive-plant,** has similar leaves but *tiny blossoms.*

BROOM
Pea Family

This introduction from the Old World suggests a *spineless* Gorse (see above). The pea-like yellow flowers are similar, but this plant has *small leaflets* that line the angled stems singly or in 3's. The seedpods are much longer than those of the Gorse. This alien, which blooms in May and June, is local from Nova Scotia and Maine southward, mainly near the coast.

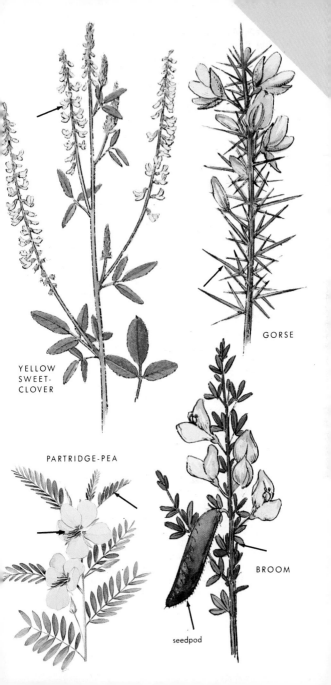

YELLOW
SWEET-
CLOVER

GORSE

PARTRIDGE-PEA

BROOM

seedpod

CANADA LILY
Lily Family

Sometimes called the Wild Yellow Lily, this attractive flower with its *nodding yellow or orange bells* sometimes occurs in a *red* form. The leaves are usually *in whorls* around the stem. Canada Lily blooms from June to August, each flower lasting 7 to 10 days. It is found in moist meadows, bogs, and sunny woodland openings.

WOOD LILY
Lily Family

Unlike most of the other spotted lilies, which nod, the Wood Lily *lifts* its orange or scarlet cup toward the sky. The leaves of the eastern form are in whorls around the stem; the leaves of the midwestern form are scattered along the stem. Look for this lily in early summer in the sandy or acid soil of meadows and woodland openings. The Day-lily (next) also has upward-facing flowers but *lacks spots*. It has swordlike leaves.

DAY-LILY
Lily Family

This spectacular lily, which originated in Asia, escaped from our gardens and now lines the roadsides in many parts of the Northeast with its tawny blossoms. The large, *upward-facing* orange flowers, which bloom from June to August, *lack the spots* which our native lilies exhibit and, as the name implies, bloom for only a day. The leaves are *long and swordlike*.

TURK'S-CAP LILY
Lily Family

This attractive native lily may be told from the Canada Lily (which is usually more yellow) by its larger, *completely reflexed petals* that form a "Turk's cap." Note the *green central star* and the *very long, projecting stamens*. Standing 3 to 8 feet tall, this lily blooms in meadows and moist ground during July and August.

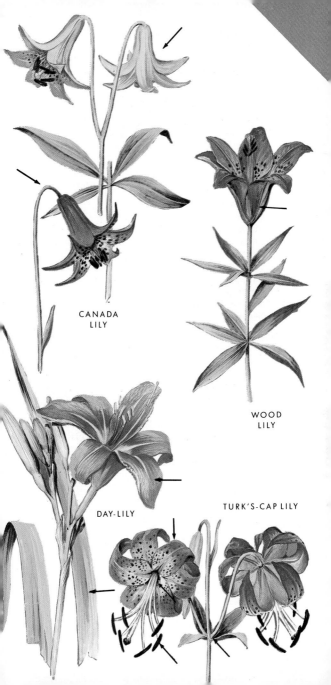

CANADA
LILY

WOOD
LILY

DAY-LILY

TURK'S-CAP LILY

TRUMPET-CREEPER
Bignonia Family

This spectacular vine, which clambers over thickets and even trees, has swollen, *trumpetlike flowers* 3 inches deep that are much favored by hummingbirds during the summer. The compound leaves are divided into 7 to 11 *toothed leaflets.* Although originally found in the thickets and woodland edges of the South, north to Illinois, Pennsylvania, and New Jersey, this vine has now become naturalized as far north as Michigan and Connecticut.

SPOTTED TOUCH-ME-NOT
Touch-me-not Family

"Jewelweed," another name, refers to the *small, spotted blossoms* which *hang by threadlike stems,* like pendant jewels. If broken, the succulent stems exude a copious juice. The small, tubular, oval seedpods, when fully ripe, split open and *pop* their seeds at a touch. In late summer these rather delicate plants come into bloom in wet shady places. **Pale Touch-me-not** (not shown) has larger yellow flowers with shorter spurs.

BUTTERFLY-WEED
Milkweed Family

The *flat-topped clusters* of orange flowers of this spectacular milkweed come into bloom in June and persist through much of the summer, attracting passing butterflies. Each individual flower, with its *flared-back petals* and *central crown,* is constructed so that a butterfly or a bee must pollinate the plant if it partakes of the nectar. A variable plant, it may be less than a foot tall in open sandy soil, 2 feet tall in grassy fields. The *seedpods,* 4 to 5 inches long, are more *spindle-shaped* than the warty pods of the Common Milkweed (see p. 95). The hairy stems are *not milky* when broken.

TRUMPET-CREEPER

SPOTTED TOUCH-ME-NOT

BUTTERFLY-
WEED

RED TRILLIUM
Lily Family

In the trilliums, *all parts*—leaves, petals, and sepals—*are in 3's.* In this species, sometimes also called "Wakerobin," the *liver-red flower* is on a *short stalk* above the broad leaves. It is one of the flowers that gives so much glory to spring in the rich woodlands of the Northeast and the Appalachians. The Red Trillium may occasionally come in other tints—pink, salmon, greenish, or white.

PAINTED TRILLIUM
Lily Family

A bit smaller than the White and Red Trilliums, this lovely inhabitant of the spring woodlands displays a *crimson blaze* at the base of its wavy white petals. Blooming from April to early June, it prefers acid woods and bogs, not the richer woodlands favored by the White and Red Trilliums.

MOCCASIN-FLOWER, PINK LADY'S-SLIPPER
Orchid Family

The *heavily veined, deeply cleft pouch or "slipper"* is usually purplish pink, but can be white. Note the *2 broad basal leaves,* which have given rise to another name, "Stemless Lady's-slipper." A resident of acid woodlands and bogs, this wild orchid blooms in May and June. Refrain from picking it; this plant takes far too long to regenerate and is endangered in many areas, as are most other orchids.

SHOWY LADY'S-SLIPPER
Orchid Family

This is our largest and most beautiful orchid, a favorite of many. The white sepals and petals are in striking contrast to the *rose-mouthed "slipper."* The large leaves *climb* the stout hairy stem. It blooms in June and July in bogs and damp woods in Canada, the border states, and southward locally in the mountains. Do not pick it.

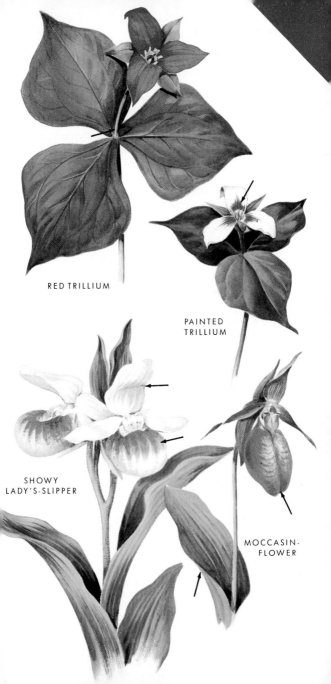

RED TRILLIUM

PAINTED
TRILLIUM

SHOWY
LADY'S-SLIPPER

MOCCASIN-
FLOWER

WILD COLUMBINE
Buttercup Family

This *nodding red and yellow flower* has 5 *hollow spurs* that point upward. Because of this and the fact that the cluster of yellow stamens points downward, any long-tongued insect or thin-billed hummingbird that wants nectar must come from below. The leaves are divided and subdivided into 3's. This wildflower blooms from April to July in rocky open woods and slopes.

CARDINAL-FLOWER
Bluebell Family

During the latter half of summer a *slender spike* of intense scarlet flowers standing 2 to 4 feet tall compels our attention along streambanks and in wet swampy places. Notice the *arrangement of petals and spurs* in the illustration. The Cardinal-flower, as we might surmise from its design and color, is a favorite of hummingbirds.

BEE-BALM, OSWEGO-TEA
Mint Family

The cluster of tubular flowers forms a *scarlet pompom.* The leaves are in pairs along the square stem. Originally found from Michigan and New York south in the Appalachians, Bee-balm was planted in gardens in New England, where it escaped and colonized new terrain. Blooming from July to September, it is a favorite of hummingbirds, as are certain other long-spurred or long-tubed scarlet flowers. The Oswego Indians once used the leaves for tea.

WILD BERGAMOT
Mint Family

The Bergamot blooms during July and August, forming extensive patches in thickets and clearings, mainly in the Appalachians. Its *pale lavender pompoms* are shaped like those of the Bee-balm. **Purple Bergamot** has *red-purple* flowers and purplish bracts. It is often cultivated.

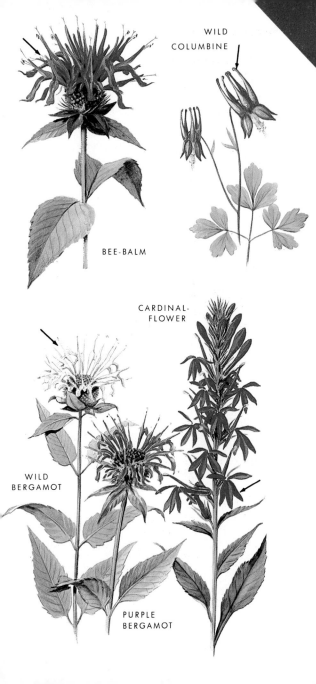

BEE-BALM

WILD
COLUMBINE

CARDINAL-
FLOWER

WILD
BERGAMOT

PURPLE
BERGAMOT

PASTURE ROSE
Rose Family

There are many kinds of wild roses—20 grow in our area. *A Field Guide to the Wildflowers* shows a selection. The attractive Pasture Rose can be told by its *slender straight prickles;* in most of the others the thorns are recurved or slightly hooked. It blooms in June or July, in sandy or rocky pastures and open woods.

SWAMP ROSE-MALLOW
Mallow Family

In late summer the most spectacular flower of the coastal marshes bursts into bloom. The Swamp Rose-mallow, with its *large, pink, hollyhock-like blossoms,* has no peers. Like other mallows, it has the characteristic *long central style,* tipped with 5 round stigmas. Standing 5 to 7 feet tall, the Rose-mallow tops the reeds in the brackish and salt marshes along the coast from southern New England to North Carolina, and locally in some freshwater marshes around the Great Lakes.

MUSK MALLOW
Mallow Family

This small, pinkish lavender mallow can be recognized by its notched petals and intricately cut leaves. As in other mallows, there is a style, or center column of stamens. An alien from the Old World, this plant has established itself widely along our roadsides, field edges, and vacant lots, where it blooms from June to September.

WILD GERANIUM
Geranium Family

This springtime favorite blooms from April to June in open woods and along shady roadsides. The hairy leaves are *deeply cleft* into 5 parts. The flower, with its 5 rose-like petals, has at its center a *long beak,* or "crane's bill." A number of less conspicuous members of the family can be identified as cranesbills by this slender beak.

PASTURE
ROSE

SWAMP
ROSE-MALLOW

MUSK MALLOW

WILD
GERANIUM

DENSE BLAZING-STAR
Daisy Family

Blazing-stars grow in open places, most of them on the prairies. There are 18 species in our area; we show only one. Blazing-stars grow in *crowded spikes;* their tufted rose-purple flowerheads are supported by scaly bracts. This species is usually hairless and has many *densely clustered,* stalkless flowerheads. The bracts are long, blunt, sticky, purple, or edged with purple. Look for this flower from July to September.

STEEPLEBUSH
Rose Family

The *steeple-like shape* of the fuzzy magenta flowerhead gives this woody shrub its name. The tiny, 5-petaled flowers bloom during July and August, starting from the top downward. The leaves, *woolly brownish* on the underside, are distinctive. Steeple-bush grows locally at the edges of meadows and pastures.

PURPLE or SPIKED LOOSESTRIFE
Loosestrife Family

This introduction from Europe carpets many of our swampy meadows with magenta during the summer. The small, *6-petaled* flowers form *slender spikes.* The downy leaves that clasp the stem are usually in pairs opposite each other, but sometimes in 3's. This alien now creates quite a show in many of our wet meadows and marsh edges, from southern Canada to the central U.S.

SHOWY TICK-TREFOIL
Pea Family

Tick-trefoils have *3-parted,* cloverlike *leaves* of various shapes. The jointed seedpods adhere to clothing and are often called *sticktights.* The lavender-purple, *pea-like blossoms* are borne in long clusters at the summit of hairy, leafy stems. This tick-trefoil, the most showy species, blooms in July and August in wood edges and open woods.

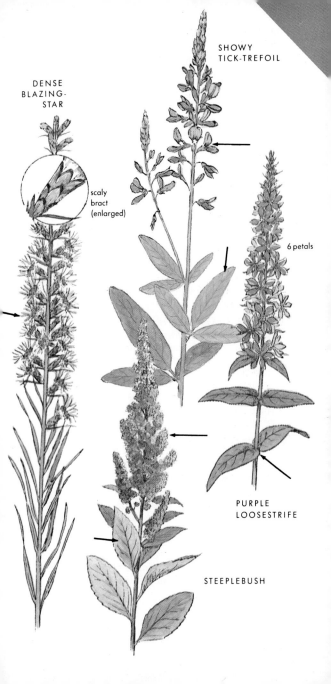

DENSE
BLAZING-
STAR

scaly
bract
(enlarged)

SHOWY
TICK-TREFOIL

6 petals

PURPLE
LOOSESTRIFE

STEEPLEBUSH

GARDEN or FALL PHLOX
Phlox Family

This well-known cultivated phlox does not usually come into bloom until summer is half over. The 5 *roundish petals* and *long corolla tube* identify this as a phlox rather than the Dame's Rocket , which it somewhat resembles. Unlike Dame's Rocket it is native, originally found in woods and thickets from Iowa and central New York south. Planted in gardens, it escaped and is now found elsewhere.

DAME'S ROCKET
Mustard Family

This pretty garden escape, originally from Europe, resembles the Garden Phlox, but note the *4 petals* (not 5). This and the *upward-pointing seedpods* indicate that it belongs to the mustard family. Blooming in May and June before the Garden Phlox comes into flower, Dame's Rocket can be pink, purple, or white.

HAIRY WILLOW-HERB
Evening-primrose Family

This beautiful alien resembles its relative, our native Fireweed (next), but most leaves are paired, and *sharply toothed.* It also differs in its *hairy* aspect and more deeply *notched petals.* It blooms during the latter half of summer, along streams and ditches.

FIREWEED
Evening-primrose Family

Tall spikes of magenta-pink flowers decorate the clearings and slopes of the uplands from the subarctic to the mountains of Georgia. In areas desolated by fire, this plant is one of the first pioneers, covering the blackened earth with a riot of bloom. The flowers have *4 round petals* that open progressively from the bottom of the flower spike. The buds above droop downward; the *seedpods point upward.*

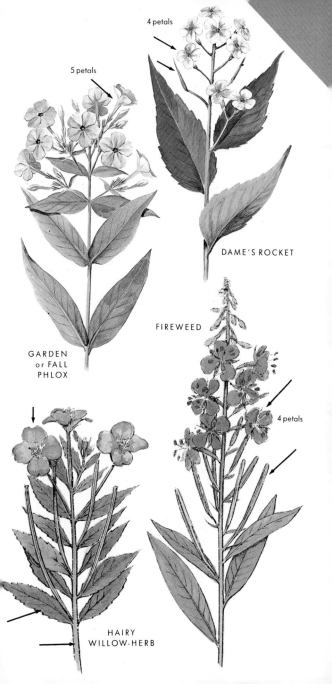

5 petals

4 petals

DAME'S ROCKET

FIREWEED

GARDEN
or FALL
PHLOX

4 petals

HAIRY
WILLOW-HERB

HEPATICA
Buttercup Family
Among the flowers of early spring, none are more loved than the hepaticas. The flowers, shining up from hairy stalks 4 to 7 inches tall, can be white, pink, lavender, or blue. The *6 to 10 "petals"* (really sepals), are supported by 3 hairy bracts. Hepaticas come in 2 forms: the **Round-lobed Hepatica** (shown here), with *rounded* leaf lobes; and the **Sharp-lobed Hepatica** (not shown), with *pointed* lobes. Both live in leafy woods, blooming in March and April before the trees leaf out, but the Sharp-lobed Hepatica prefers a more upland habitat.

COMMON WOOD-SORREL
Wood-sorrel Family
Wood-sorrels *(Oxalis)* have cloverlike or *shamrocklike* leaves, divided into 3 heart-shaped leaflets. In this species the 5 white or pink petals are *strongly veined with pink.* Scarcely 3 or 4 inches high, it graces the woodland floor in June and July in Canada, the northern edge of the U.S., and southward in the Appalachians.

CAROLINA SPRING-BEAUTY
Purslane Family
This little flower of the spring woods is similar to the Spring-beauty (see below and p. 19) except for its broader, *paddle-shaped leaves.* In spite of its name, it is found in the Appalachians northward to southern Canada and westward.

SPRING-BEAUTY
Purslane Family
This well-named denizen of the woods has white or pink petals with darker pink veins. It is identified by the pair of smooth, *grasslike leaves* midway on the stem. Blooming from March to May in the woods and uplands, it can be confused only with the Carolina Spring-beauty (see above and p. 19).

ROUND-LOBED
HEPATICA

COMMON
WOOD-SORREL

CAROLINA
SPRING-BEAUTY

SPRING-
BEAUTY

FRINGED POLYGALA, GAYWINGS
Milkwort Family

The rather *oval, evergreen leaves* suggest those of the Wintergreen and for this reason it is sometimes called the "Flowering Wintergreen." The flowers, surprisingly suggestive of little orchids, have *2 flaring, pink-purple "wings,"* which are really sepals. The true petals are united into a tube, which is tipped with a *bushy fringe.* The flowering stalk, 3 to 6 inches tall, springs from a prostrate underground stem. Fringed Polygala blooms in May and June in the woodlands of Canada, the northeastern U.S., and southward in the Appalachians.

TWINFLOWER
Honeysuckle Family

This dainty creeping plant of the woodlands sends up its fragrant *pairs of small, pink, nodding bells* on 3- to 6-inch stalks. The leaves, clustered near the base of the flower stalk, are small and roundish. Summer (June to August) is the time of bloom in the cooler woods of Canada southward to the Great Lakes states and the mountains of West Virginia.

TRAILING ARBUTUS
Heath Family

The *oval, leathery leaves* of this low creeping plant of the woodlands remain green over winter and can be spotted against the dead brown tree leaves, among which their trailing hairy stems are rooted. This is one of the first flowers to appear in the spring, blooming from March to May. The clusters of small pink or white blossoms expand from a short tube into 5 flaring lobes. Trailing Arbutus, a true harbinger of spring, is found in the sandy or acid soils of forests and woodlots from Canada southward across the eastern U.S.

FRINGED POLYGALA

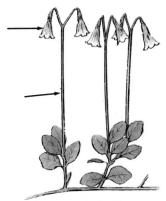

TWINFLOWER

TRAILING
ARBUTUS

SWEET JOE-PYE-WEED
Daisy Family

The fuzzy, pale, pinkish purple flowers form a massive, somewhat dome-shaped cluster. The stem, usually *green* with a slight whitish bloom, is *purplish or blackish* at the leaf joints. The leaves, usually *in whorls of 3 or 4*, have a sweetish odor when crushed, rather like vanilla. Found in thickets and woods, Sweet Joe-Pye-weed blooms throughout much of the East during the latter half of the summer. There are several similar species of Joe-Pye-weed (see below).

SPOTTED JOE-PYE-WEED
Daisy Family

This attractive plant, with its fuzzy, pink-purple flowers, is similar to the Sweet Joe-Pye-weed but the stem is *deep purple,* or *spotted* with purple. The flower clusters, of a deeper color, are *more flat-topped,* less domed. The leaves are *in whorls of 4 or 5.* Spotted Joe-Pye-weed blooms in late summer in wet thickets and meadows. The **Hollow Joe-Pye-weed** (not shown), is somewhat like the other two, but the stem is *hollow,* and although it is tinged with purple, it is seldom spotted. It may have more leaves (4 to 7) in each whorl.

SALT-MARSH FLEABANE
Daisy Family

In late summer, from southern Maine south, a sticky, camphor-smelling plant tinges the salt marshes along the coast with pink-purple. Although it belongs to the Composite or Daisy Family, it *lacks petal-like rays* around the flowerheads, which are in *flattish terminal clusters.* The alternate leaves are slightly toothed. Primarily a coastal plant, it is rarely found inland.

SWEET
JOE-PYE-WEED

SPOTTED
JOE-PYE-WEED

SALT-MARSH
FLEABANE

CROSS-LEAVED MILKWORT
Milkwort Family

The *tight, oblong,* purplish red (or greenish white) *flowerhead* suggests a clover, but the narrow leaves do not; they are *in whorls of 4, forming crosses* around the stem. This low plant, only 4 to 10 inches tall, blooms from July to October in sandy soil, bogs, pinelands, and marsh edges along the coast from Maine southward and locally inland from Minnesota and Ohio southward.

RED CLOVER
Pea Family

The familiar Red Clover, an alien from Europe, is now quite happy in our fields and waysides. Each leaflet of the tripartite leaves usually shows a *pale chevron.* The Red Clover blooms from May throughout the summer. **Zigzag Clover** (not shown), is similar to the Red Clover but the flowers are *more deeply colored* and the slender leaflets *lack* the chevrons. The stem is often zigzag. **Rabbit's-foot Clover** (not shown) is a smaller clover with small silky leaves and soft, *fuzzy, grayish pink* flowerheads. It is another alien to look for along roadsides and in waste places throughout our area.

PURPLE GERARDIA
Snapdragon Family

Gerardias have *pairs of pink-purple, bell-like flowers* in the axils of the upper leaves. There are 18 kinds in our area and to recognize some of them the botanist must become quite technical. The one shown here, the largest, has downy flowers on *very short stalks.* It blooms in late summer (August to September) in damp, acidic soils and wet meadows as far north as Minnesota, southern Michigan, Ohio, New York, and southern New England.

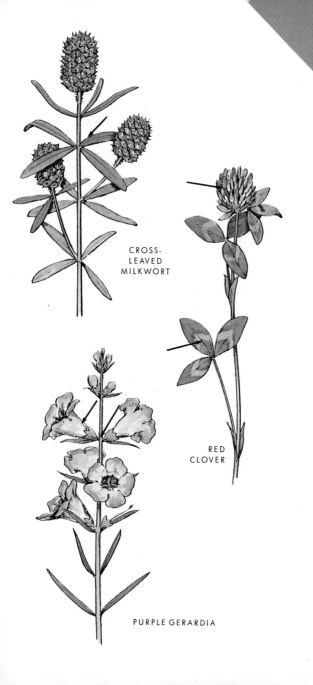

CROSS-
LEAVED
MILKWORT

RED
CLOVER

PURPLE GERARDIA

COMMON MILKWEED
Milkweed Family

The *unique flower structure, long pointed seedpods,* and the thick *milky juice* of the broken stems and leaves are typical of the milkweeds. This species can be told from the various other milkweeds by the *warty* aspect of the gray-green seedpods. The rounded flower clusters, mostly in the leaf axils, vary in subtle shades of dusty rose and lavender. This species prefers the dry soil of roadsides and fields, where it blooms from June to August, attracting many butterflies. The Monarch, whose larvae feed on the noxious leaves, thereby gains immunity from predation by birds.

SWAMP MILKWEED
Milkweed Family

Unlike the Common Milkweed, which is a stout *downy* plant, the Swamp Milkweed is *smooth,* with relatively *narrow, lance-shaped leaves.* The pink flowers are smaller, clustered in relatively small umbels. It blooms during the same summer weeks as the Common Milkweed, but prefers swamps and wet ground.

WOOD-BETONY
Snapdragon Family

This curious flower also goes by the unattractive name of "Lousewort." It is a short, hairy plant, 5 to 14 inches high, topped by a *whorl of tubular, snapdragon-like flowers;* these may be red, yellow, or both. The *slender, finely cut leaves,* mostly basal, are often reddish in color. A spring flower, Wood-betony blooms from April to June in wood edges and clearings from southern Canada and Maine southward to the Gulf states. The name "Lousewort" comes from the belief once held by farmers that cattle or sheep became infested with lice when grazing on these plants.

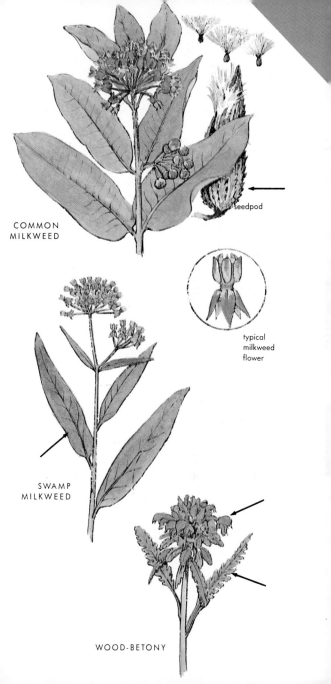

COMMON
MILKWEED

seedpod

typical
milkweed
flower

SWAMP
MILKWEED

WOOD-BETONY

LADY'S-THUMB
Buckwheat Family

Smartweeds (there are a number of kinds) are known by their *tight, spikelike clusters* of tiny pink or whitish flowers and their "knotted" stems, with a papery sheath at each joint. Lady's-thumb has narrow leaves, often with a *dark triangular blotch.* The stems are *reddish,* giving rise to its other name—"Redleg." This alien weed is widespread in cultivated ground and waste places throughout our area. **Pale Smartweed** (not shown), a native plant, is similar, but the stems are usually *green* and the flower clusters are paler, with *bent tips.*

SWAMP SMARTWEED
Buckwheat Family

The Swamp Smartweed can take many forms; it may be erect when growing on the swampy margins of ponds, or it may have floating leaves when rooted in the water; in addition, intermediate forms may reflect varying water levels. The Swamp Smartweed has *longer flowerheads* than most of the related smartweeds. Look for it during the summer months in swamps, shallow water, ditches, and along the shores throughout most of our area.

WATER SMARTWEED
Buckwheat Family

This Smartweed, which grows in swamps, shallow water, and ditches, is as plastic and variable in its leaf shape and manner of growth as the Swamp Smartweed. The quick way to tell the two apart is by the flower cluster, which in this species is *stubby, usually less than an inch long,* quite in contrast to the more slim flower-heads of the other species. A number of other kinds of smartweeds may be distinguished by technical characters.

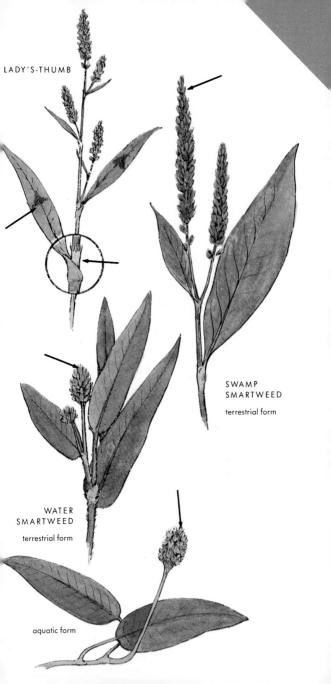

LADY'S-THUMB

SWAMP
SMARTWEED

terrestrial form

WATER
SMARTWEED

terrestrial form

aquatic form

TEASEL
Teasel Family

This curious plant looks like an *egg-shaped pincushion* perched atop a prickly stem. The minute lavender florets are packed between the spines of the flowerhead. The *slender, paired leaves* embrace the stem. The dried flowerheads, which persist on the dead stems throughout the winter, are sometimes used in home decoration. This alien plant, blooming from July to October, can be found locally along roadsides and in waste ground from Michigan, Ontario, and western New England southward.

SPOTTED KNAPWEED
Daisy Family

Although their flowerheads look like those of thistles, the many kinds of knapweeds *lack prickles or spines.* The Spotted Knapweed—perhaps the most familiar and widespread species—can be either pink, purple, or white. The flower *bracts* supporting the flowerheads have *fringed black triangular tips.* The majority of knapweeds are alien; this one lines our roadsides and field edges in many places from June to August.

COMMON BURDOCK
Daisy Family

Sooner or later, everyone becomes familiar with this thistle-like plant and its burs that stick persistently to clothing. The *roundish burs* support tiny lavender florets during the time of bloom, which extends from July to October. The lower leaves are large, with hollow stalks. The Burdock, an alien, is found widely along roadsides and in waste places. A larger species, the **Great Burdock** (not shown), has much larger burs that are supported on *long stalks.*

TEASEL

SPOTTED
KNAPWEED

COMMON
BURDOCK

SWAMP THISTLE
Daisy Family

There are many kinds of thistles, some with more spines or prickles than others. This one blooms from July to September in swamps, wet woods, and thickets. It has *no spines* on its *hollow stem* and the *bracts* are not tipped with spines but are *sticky*. The deeply incised leaves near the base form a rosette. Although usually purplish, the flowers can be white.

BULL THISTLE
Daisy Family

If you see a thistle with a *full, large flowerhead* it is most likely this species, a showy alien that is often found in our fields and along the roadsides. To confirm the identification, look for the rigid, yellow-tipped *spines* of the bracts that support the flowerhead. The prickly leaves are pale or woolly beneath. The handsome, reddish purple flowers decorate the landscape from June to September. The **Pasture Thistle** (not shown) is also called the "Bull Thistle." It is a native, even larger than the alien Bull Thistle. The *very hairy stems lack the prickly wings*, and the spines on the leaves are very long.

CANADA THISTLE
Daisy Family

Although this *small, multi-headed* thistle is a native of Europe, where it goes by the name of Creeping Thistle, inexplicably it is known on this side of the Atlantic as the Canada Thistle. The flowerheads are *small*—scarcely more than half an inch across. Usually they are pale lilac; rarely they may be white. This, our most common and widespread thistle, blooms in the fields, pastures, and roadsides during the latter half of summer, from July to September.

SWAMP
THISTLE

BULL
THISTLE

CANADA
THISTLE

NEW ENGLAND ASTER
Daisy Family

Of the many kinds of asters that bloom across the land during late summer and autumn, this is the most showy. In some places, especially around the Great Lakes, the roadsides and meadows are literally purple with masses of these attractive flowers, which are often cultivated in various horticultural forms, ranging from blue-purple to magenta. The numerous *toothless leaves clasp the hairy stem.* Blooming from August to October, it lends its beauty to the countryside from southern Canada to the uplands of the Carolinas. When the Monarch Butterfly migrates south, it often satisfies its thirst with the nectar of this flower.

NEW YORK ASTER
Daisy Family

There are many kinds of asters, whose flowers range in color from blue to violet. These can be subdivided into those whose *leaves do or do not clasp the stem.* This one has *narrowly lanceolate leaves* that are *not* deeply clasping and which may or may not have toothed edges. The flowers are deep violet, similar in hue to those of the New England Aster, but the stem is *smooth or only slightly hairy.* New York Aster blooms in late summer and autumn in wet meadows and on shores, mainly along the seacoast.

LARGE-LEAVED ASTER
Daisy Family

Note the *very large basal leaves,* which may be 4 to 8 inches wide; the upper leaves are small. The flower rays are violet (or white) and the central disk becomes reddish as the season advances. The flowering branches are rather *sticky.* Look for this aster in woods and clearings from Minnesota and maritime Canada southward to the Great Lakes states and in the mountains to North Carolina.

NEW YORK ASTER

NEW ENGLAND ASTER

LARGE-LEAVED ASTER

BLUE LETTUCE
Daisy Family

There are a number of kinds of wild lettuce, which (being so tall) do not look at all like the lowly lettuce of the garden. Some are blue, some yellow, some white. The small flowers *in loose panicles* (clusters) are asterlike, but the leaves are more dandelionlike. The several blue kinds vary a good deal in *leaf shape* and other features. They may stand taller than a man—6 to 8 feet—or even 10 feet or more. Look for these *tall, gangly plants* in moist thickets or along shady roads during late summer and early fall.

CHICORY
Daisy Family

This alien that grows so commonly in the sterile ground along our road shoulders is much too pretty to be dismissed as a "weed." The clear blue flowers that hug the nearly naked stems wilt and surrender their beauty by midday. If you look at the base of the wiry stems you will note some dandelionlike leaves. Chicory blooms from June to October, and although it is usually blue, it may often be white, and rarely pink.

ROBIN-PLANTAIN
Daisy Family

Blooming in spring, from April to June, the Robin-plantain is one of the fleabanes (see also p. 38). Superficially it looks like an aster, but need not be mistaken for one because asters are strictly flowers of late summer and autumn. The numerous rays, pale violet to magenta, surround a rather large central disk. At the base of the plant is a cluster of broad fuzzy leaves. Look for the Robin-plantain in open woods and fields as far north as southern Canada.

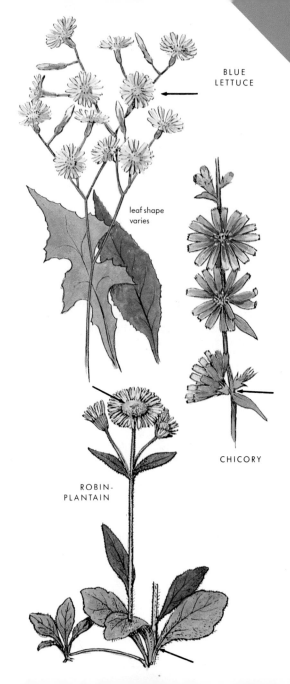

BLUE
LETTUCE

leaf shape
varies

CHICORY

ROBIN-
PLANTAIN

LARGER BLUE FLAG
Iris Family

The Blue Flag, or "Wild Iris," is a wild relative of the garden irises. Standing 2 to 3 feet tall, it is one of our most elegant wildflowers. Graceful, *swordlike leaves* flank the slender stalk that supports a showy violet flower with erect petals and broad, heavily veined, down-curved sepals. Blooming from May to July in marshes and wet meadows, this iris ranges across southern Canada, the adjacent border states, and southward in the mountains to Virginia. The **Slender Blue Flag** (not shown) has *narrower, more grasslike leaves.* It replaces the Larger Blue Flag in marshes near the coast.

SPIDERWORT
Spiderwort Family

Three *roundish violet petals* accented by golden stamens, and the long, iris-like leaves, characterize the Spiderwort, which is often cultivated for its exotic beauty. It blooms from April to July along roadsides, thicket edges, and in woodland margins from Minnesota, Wisconsin, and Maine south. The **Ohio Spiderwort** (not shown) of the Midwest has *smooth*, not hairy, flower stalks and bracts. There are several other species of spiderworts, found mostly in the prairie states.

ASIATIC DAYFLOWER
Spiderwort Family

In dayflowers the *upper 2 petals* are *larger* than the lower one which supports the curved stamens. There are several kinds. The one shown here is an alien that has established itself in waste places and along our roadsides, where it blooms from June to October. It can be told from our native **Virginia Dayflower** (not shown) by the small *lower petal*, which is *white* in this species, not *blue.*

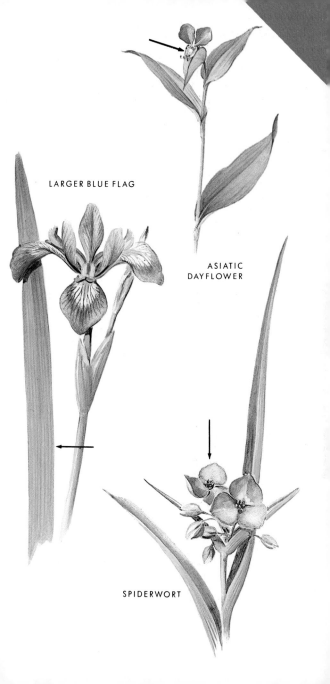

LARGER BLUE FLAG

ASIATIC
DAYFLOWER

SPIDERWORT

VIPER'S BUGLOSS
Forget-me-not Family

It is surprising to learn that this rather vulgar, *bristly* roadside plant belongs to the same family as the dainty Forget-me-not. It is another of those imports from the Old World which feels comfortable along some of the road shoulders and waste places on this side of the Atlantic. The blue flowers with their *projecting red stamens* bloom one at a time on each of the *short, curved flower branchlets* that climb the upper stalk. Viper's Bugloss blooms from June to September.

GREAT LOBELIA
Bluebell Family

There are many kinds of blue lobelias. As a group they are known by their *flower structure*, with 2 narrow lobes or "ears" above, and 3 wider lobes forming a lip below. This, the largest and most showy species, is *striped with white* on the lower lobes and on the underside or "belly" of the corolla. Its tall spikes bloom during August and September, often making quite a show in swampy places and wet ground from Manitoba to western New England and south.

PICKERELWEED
Pickerelweed Family

The Pickerelweed raises *tight clubs of small blue flowers* above its glossy, *arrowhead-shaped leaves*. It blooms throughout the summer months from June to October, forming emergent gardens in shallow water at the edges of quiet ponds and sluggish streams, often in association with water-lilies and arrowheads. As you might guess, pickerel often lurk in the same muddy waters where this attractive plant takes root. The nutlike seeds are edible and the young leaf stalks, often eaten by deer, can be cooked as greens.

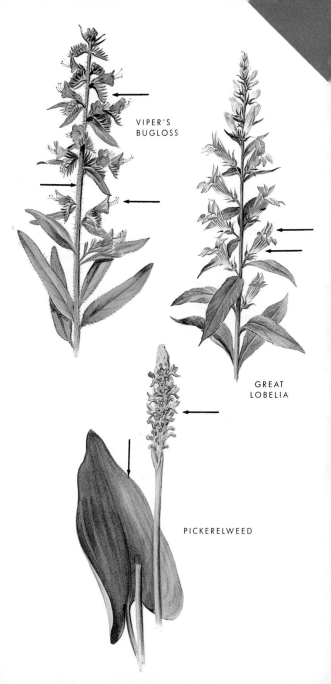

VIPER'S
BUGLOSS

GREAT
LOBELIA

PICKERELWEED

COMMON BLUE VIOLET
Violet Family

Violets have a distinctive flower shape; they resemble pansies in miniature. They are 5-petaled with the 2 upper petals raised, the 2 side ones drooping. The bottom petal is wider, heavily veined, and extends back into a short spur. The leaves rise separately from the same base as the flowers. Violets may bloom as early as March but are at their best in April and May. In the Common Blue Violet (shown here) *all 3* lower petals are strongly veined. It is found in damp woods and meadows north to Minnesota, Ohio, and New York state.

MARSH BLUE VIOLET
Violet Family

This violet, a bit larger than the Common Blue Violet, prefers wet meadows, springs, and bogs. Its flowers are on stems that are taller than the heart-shaped leaves. The petals are *darker toward the throat;* the lower petal is *shorter.* It blooms from April to June throughout much of our area, but mostly in the uplands southward. The leaves of violets are the foodplants of the caterpillars of Fritillary butterflies.

BIRDFOOT VIOLET
Violet Family

Although most blue violets have heart-shaped leaves, in this species the leaves are *finely segmented* into 9 to 15 points. One variety has *uniformly colored* petals; another is *bicolored,* with its 2 upper petals darker than the three lower ones. Birdfoot Violet is local, but should be looked for in dry sandy fields and other sunny places from Minnesota, Michigan, southern Ontario, and Massachusetts south.

Note: There are many other kinds of blue violets, most of them with heart-shaped leaves; 15 are described in *A Field Guide to Wildflowers of Northeastern and North-central North America.*

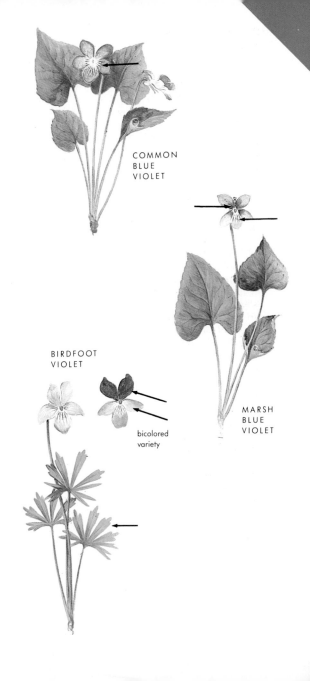

COMMON
BLUE
VIOLET

MARSH
BLUE
VIOLET

BIRDFOOT
VIOLET

bicolored
variety

FRINGED GENTIAN
Gentian Family

The flowers of the many kinds of blue gentians are erect and vaselike. Some flare open, others remain closed. In the Fringed Gentian, the 4 *delicately fringed petals* flare out from the deep corolla tube. This gentian blooms late, from September to November, favoring meadows, banks, and wet woodland openings. It can be found locally across southern Canada and the northern states and southward in the mountains to Georgia.

CLOSED GENTIAN
Gentian Family

In this relative of the better-known Fringed Gentian the blue-purple petals remain *closed,* hence its other name, "Bottle Gentian." Several of the tubular, erect flowers are clustered at the tip of the 1- to 2-foot stem. The Closed Gentian is a late summer plant, blooming from August to October in meadows and other wet places from southern Canada and Vermont southward. The **Stiff Gentian** (not shown) is smaller, with a *tight cluster* of erect lavender flowers that are tipped with 5 bristle-pointed lobes. It is found mainly in the Appalachian Mountains.

TALL BELLFLOWER
Bluebell Family

Unlike some other members of the bluebell family, this species does not have bells. Instead, the 5-lobed flowers are *flat and starlike,* light blue with a paler ring at the center. The *long, recurved style* is distinctive. Tall Bellflower blooms during the summer, from June to August, in the rich soil of banks and thickets from Minnesota, southern Ontario, and New York state southward.

FRINGED
GENTIAN

CLOSED GENTIAN

TALL BELLFLOWER

BLUE PHLOX
Phlox Family

Carpets of these pale violet flowers brighten the woodland floor when trees are putting out new leaves and the warblers are migrating north. The pinwheel cluster of *5-petaled flowers* radiates from the tip of a sticky 18-inch stem. The Blue Phlox blooms from April to June in rich open woods.

VIRGINIA WATERLEAF
Waterleaf Family

The *terminal clusters of bell-like, violet or white flowers* suggest those of Greek Valerian (below), but note the very different *leaves.* Virginia Waterleaf blooms from May to August in rich woods from Manitoba to western New England and southward. A related species, the **Appendaged Waterleaf** (not shown) has *broader,* somewhat *maple-like* leaves. The leaves of both are often marked as though they were stained with water; hence the name.

MERTENSIA, VIRGINIA COWSLIP
Forget-me-not Family

When the nodding, blue, trumpetlike flowers are *in bud they are pink.* The oval leaves are *strongly veined* and smooth; the stem is smooth and succulent. This springtime beauty blooms from March to May, sometimes forming great beds in the moist bottomlands and woods along rivers from Minnesota, southern Ontario, and New York south. It is sometimes cultivated in gardens.

GREEK VALERIAN
Phlox Family

The *delicate blue bells* and the intricate leaves, divided into *5 to 15 paired leaflets,* identify this frail beauty of the spring woods from Minnesota to New York and southward. A similar plant, **Jacob's-ladder** (not shown) has *more leaflets* (15 to 19), in ladderlike pairs, and the *stamens protrude* from the flowers.

5 petals

BLUE PHLOX

VIRGINIA WATERLEAF

MERTENSIA

GREEK VALERIAN

TRUE FORGET-ME-NOT
Forget-me-not Family

The flowers, growing on 2 diverging branches, are *sky blue* with a *yellow eye.* This pretty little flower favors wet places and brooksides rather than the roadsides and waste places occupied by most other alien plants. The blooming season extends from May to October. There are several other alien forget-me-nots in our area, as well as the **Smaller Forget-me-not** (not shown), which is native.

BLUE-EYED GRASS
Iris Family

These modest little blue-eyed flowers belong to the same family as the flamboyant blue flags or irises (see p. 107). There are a number of kinds, all much alike except for technical differences. They are *stiff, grasslike* plants with *one or two small, deep blue, 6-petaled flowers.* Each petal is tipped with a small point. The blue-eyed grasses bloom in early summer in meadows and along marsh edges and shores.

BLUETS
Bedstraw Family

Pale blue to almost white, with a yellow eye, this delicate floret establishes itself colonially on lawns and grassy places, where it forms ethereal patches of light blue against the green grass. The flowers are borne singly on slender 2- to 8-inch stems which rise in a group from a common base. The *tiny leaves* are short and slender, arranged *in pairs* along the stem. Flowering from April to June before the grass towers over it, this little blue flower has a preference for acid soils throughout much of our area.

TRUE
FORGET-ME-NOT

BLUE-EYED
GRASS

BLUETS

PEPPERMINT
Mint Family

The many kinds of mints may be recognized as a family by their *square stems* and *paired leaves.* Their small, lipped flowers, usually pink or violet, are mostly in *tight terminal clusters.* The slim Peppermint (shown here), an alien, grows widely on shores, wet meadows, and along roadsides throughout our area. Chew the leaves and note their fragrance and pungent taste. The pale purple or pink-purple flower clusters are in *short or interrupted spikes* on stems 1½ to 3 feet tall. They bloom in late summer, from July to September.

HEAL-ALL, SELFHEAL
Mint Family

This is another alien that finds our roadsides, lawns, vacant lots, and waste places to its liking. It is a short, *creeping* plant, from 3 to 12 inches tall, with *hooded violet flowers* that form a *squarish or oblong head.* It blooms all summer, from May to September, throughout our area.

BEACH PEA
Pea Family

As we walk among the dunes along the seashore in midsummer, we cannot fail to notice this attractive plant. The showy, pink-lavender, *pea-like flowers* tell us the family, and the *large arrowhead-shaped stipules* (leaflike appendages) at the base of the leaf stalks confirm the species. The Beach Pea blooms from June to August above high-tide line on sandy shores and among the dunes from New Jersey northward. It can also be found locally along the shores of the Great Lakes, Lake Champlain, and Oneida Lake.

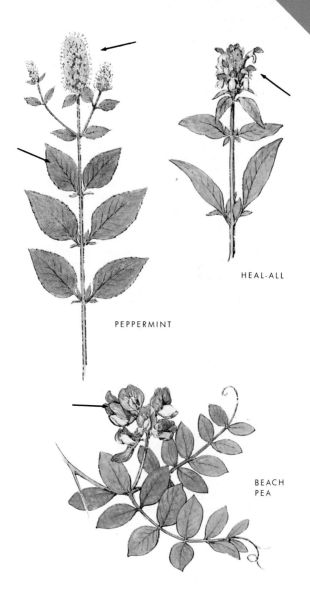

PEPPERMINT

HEAL-ALL

BEACH
PEA

PITCHER-PLANT
Pitcher-plant Family

Look for this unmistakable carnivorous plant in the sphagnum bogs of Canada and the cooler parts of the northern states as well as in coastal bogs southward. The single, nodding, dull purplish red flower rises on a leafless stalk, clasped at the base by a rosette of heavily veined, dull red or green, *pitcherlike leaves.* These are half-filled with dew or rain water. The flared mouth of the "pitcher" is lined with downward-pointing bristles that help trap insects which try to climb out. The captive insects drown and are broken down by bacterial activity and enzymes and eventually digested.

COMMON CATTAIL
Cattail Family

This slim marsh plant, growing in dense stands, dominates most freshwater marshes. The *sausage-like brown heads* of tiny, closely packed pistillate (female) flowers are distinctive. The *swordlike leaves,* 3 to 9 feet long, may form beds so thick as to conceal anyone wading through the marsh. The **Narrow-leaved Cattail** (not shown) is more typical of brackish water near the coast. It has *much narrower leaves* and the staminate flowers (the pale part) are *separated by a gap* from the pistillate (brown) flowerhead.

SKUNK CABBAGE
Arum Family

Although the Skunk Cabbage is a far cry from the pristine Calla Lily, it belongs to the same family. The *spathe (sheath)* surrounding the rounded spadix varies from green to brown and is *heavily spotted.* The flowers often appear as early as February, before the broad leaves uncoil. Step on them and a *fetid odor* leaves no doubt as to their identity. Skunk Cabbage grows in wet woods and open swamps of southern Canada and the northern states and southward in the Appalachians.

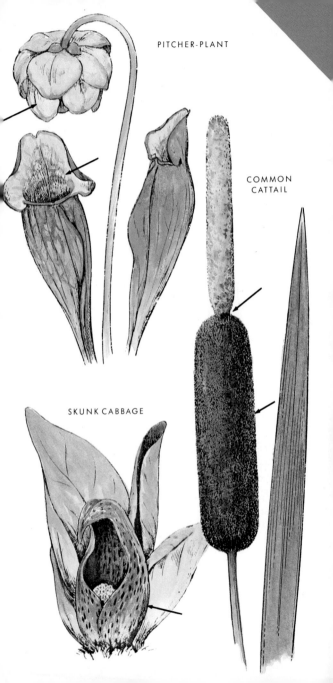

PITCHER-PLANT

COMMON
CATTAIL

SKUNK CABBAGE

JACK-IN-THE-PULPIT
Arum Family

"Jack" is the *clublike spadix* that is
ensconced like a preacher in the canopied
"pulpit" (the *spathe*), which may be
green or purplish brown. The actual flowers
are tiny and are hidden at the base of the
spadix; they develop later into a tight
cluster of scarlet berries. The *3-parted
leaves,* either one or two per plant, are on
long stalks. Blooming from April to June in
woods, swamps, and bogs, the Jack-in-
the-Pulpit comes in several varieties which
some botanists regard as separate species.
The one shown here is often known as
the **Woodland Jack-in-the-pulpit**; it usually
has *2 leaves* that are gray-green beneath.
The **Small** or **Swamp Jack-in-the-pulpit**
(not shown) is smaller, with a *single*
3-parted leaf that is bright green beneath.
It is confined more to the states along
the Atlantic Seaboard.

WILD GINGER
Birthwort Family

The *large, heart-shaped leaves* of the Wild
Ginger are a conspicuous feature of the
forest floor in the spring, but the *single,*
early-blooming flower, appearing in April
and May, goes almost unnoticed because it
is *nearly hidden* beneath the leaves at
ground level. *Cup-shaped,* with 3 reddish
brown calyx lobes, the flower is situated in
the crotch *between the hairy leaf stalks* of
the paired leaves. The habitat of this plant
is rich woodlands from Minnesota across
southeastern Canada to the Gaspé and
southward to Arkansas and North Carolina.
The roots, which have a gingerlike odor,
can be used as a confection when cooked
with sugar.

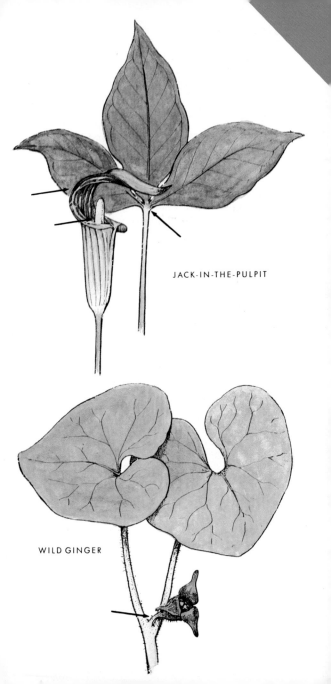

JACK-IN-THE-PULPIT

WILD GINGER

FALSE HELLEBORE
Lily Family

In early spring the large, *heavily ribbed leaves* of this plant are a conspicuous feature in wet woods and swamps. The flowering stalk, *2 to 8 feet tall,* bears a *large cluster of star-shaped flowers* which may be yellow-green at first, dull green later. These bloom from May to July in the swampy woods of southern Canada, the northern states and southward in the Appalachians to Georgia.

SOLOMON'S-SEAL
Lily Family

Unlike the False Solomon's-seal (p. 36), which bears its cluster of whitish flowers at the tip of the leafy stem, this plant, the "true" Solomon's-seal, *dangles its pairs of yellow-green flowers from the axils* of the leaves, which are spaced alternately along the stem. It blooms in May and June in woods and thickets from Illinois, Michigan, and southern Ontario, New York, and Connecticut southward. The **Great Solomon's-seal** (not shown) grows to a height of 4 to 8 feet. Its dangling flowers are usually in clusters of *more than 2.*

FALSE
HELLEBORE

SOLOMON'S-SEAL

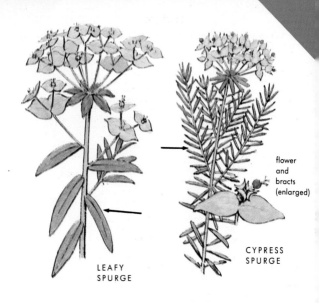

flower
and
bracts
(enlarged)

CYPRESS
SPURGE

LEAFY
SPURGE

SPURGES. There are many kinds of spurges
or euphorbias—some native, some alien. At
least a dozen have greenish flowers of the
type shown here. The 2 yellow-green
"petals" are really bracts that support the
curious tiny flowers.

LEAFY SPURGE
Spurge Family
This alien, which forms greenish patches
in the dry soil along roadsides, can be
found locally in southern Canada and the
northern U.S. It has *broader leaves*
than the next species.

CYPRESS SPURGE
Spurge Family
This is sometimes called the "Cemetery
Plant" because of its frequency in cemeteries
as well as along roadsides. Its *fine, needle-
like leaves* separate it from the previous
species. The petal-like bracts may turn red.

Index

Color illustrations of the wildflowers generally appear on the page facing the text. To avoid duplication, the illustrations are not indexed separately.